CRUSH ANXIETY
FEAR & PAIN
KEYS TO HEALING

Gail Marie King

Crush Anxiety, Fear, and Pain
Gail Marie King

eBook ISBN: 978-1-956190-02-1
Print ISBN: 978-1-956190-00-7

Published by Gail Marie King

PO Box 146766
Chicago, IL 60614-8553

This book is dedicated to God's Holy Spirit, whom I respect as the Author of God's Word, to my beloved family, and to all of God's children.

You will keep him in perfect peace,
Whose mind is stayed on You,
Because he trusts in You.

– Isaiah 26:3, NKJV

TABLE OF CONTENTS

CRUSH ANXIETY
FEAR & PAIN
KEYS TO HEALING

PREFACE

...This is what the LORD, the God of your father David, says: I have heard your prayer and seen your tears; I will heal you...

– 2 Kings 20:5, NIV

THE EPIPHANY THAT TURNED MY HEALTH AROUND

Years ago, as I lay on my sickbed, unable to sit up for more than 20 minutes at a time, I had many questions.

- Why did this happen to me?
- Why was I cut down?
- What is God saying to me?
- Should I give up and face death?
- Will I die prematurely?
- Can I recover?
- If so, how?

I tried to understand how I arrived at this point in my life. I had practiced healthy eating and natural healing modalities since my youth. However, I had to acknowledge that before this illness, I had abandoned my good habits. Now I was overeating junk foods, neglecting my sleep, and had become a workaholic.

As a result, I was in a wheelchair, unable to work, and facing two operations. To alleviate my anxiety, fear, and pain, I had a full-time homemaker. She sat with me, helped me around, cooked my meals, and cleaned the apartment.

I attended one of the best hospitals in Chicago on the medical end, and my doctors were top-notch. Nonetheless, they could only offer surgery and life-long dependence on drugs. They could not instantly cure me.

I love and respect my doctors, but they are not God.

I needed a miracle.

My only hope to live and take my life back was God. I needed divine healing. I needed a miracle.

This book was inspired because, throughout my life, I have received many miracles of divine healing. In addition, I have my own experiences as proof that Jesus Christ is still in the healing business and the Word of God is true.

HOW WE GET WELL

Looking back, I remembered that years ago, I asked God why so many of His children (in the church) were sick. Then, quickly, God said to me, "They don't know Me."

Yes, we know of God, and we pray to Him. However, the true nature of God is mainly unknown. Through the prophet Hosea, God said this.

"My people are destroyed because they don't know me"...

– Hosea 4:6, NLT

Similarly, through the prophet Isaiah, God said this.

"The ox knoweth his owner, and the ass his master's crib: but Israel doth not know, my people doth not consider."

– Isaiah 1:3, KJB

How does our lack of knowledge about God and His word impact our health? As we see in the above scriptures, God clearly says that even His children cannot survive and thrive unless we know Him intimately. Therefore, we must understand the true nature of God and the ways of God to receive divine healing.

Is it difficult or impossible to understand and apply divine healing from the Word of God? No, it isn't. We can be comforted by Jesus' words.

"Then Jesus said, "Come to me, all of you who are weary and carry heavy burdens, and I will give you rest."

– Matthew 11:28, NLT

THREE OBSTACLES WE CAN OVERCOME

During my healing journey, I noticed that we must overcome these three obstacles to have victory in our health and Christian life.

1. ANXIETY (including worry and depression)

2. FEAR

3. PAIN (physical and emotional)

To achieve divine healing, we must overcome anxiety, fear, and pain. In this book, we will focus on these three.

WHY THIS BOOK WAS WRITTEN

In the Lord's lovingkindness and mercy, He took me off a sickbed and out of a wheelchair. I was granted freedom from painful medical treatments. I returned to work, and medical bills that totaled over thirty thousand were paid off. He strengthened me and encouraged me to complete a 26.2-mile marathon.

God alone did all of this. It was miraculous!

> His miracles in my life have never ceased.

Most importantly, He called me to ministry to share His faithfulness and His miracles with others.

INTRODUCTION

> God wants us to use what we already have to become free of anxiety, fear, and pain.

*W*hen we understand what we have (in Christ), we will walk in the freedom that is ours. This is excellent news.

In this book on crushing anxiety, fear, and pain, concepts that are imperative to our success are reiterated. In this way, our precious Holy Spirit can wipe out the anxiety, fear, and pain that has ravaged our lives.

Remember, Jesus had great compassion for the sick. Most importantly, as we address anxiety, fear, and pain individually, the following themes will be explained in-depth because they are foundational to our victory.

1. Confidence in the love of God and the impact of walking in love with others

2. Speaking the Word of God over our situation

3. How faith becomes visible through our actions

4. How to think on good things, through a mind that is renewed by the healing words of God

5. How to cast out demons of anxiety, fear, and pain

As you would imagine, Jesus Christ mastered the above principles and taught us to do the same.

Heal the sick, raise the dead, cure those with leprosy, and cast out demons. Give as freely as you have received!

– Matthew 10:8, NLT

When he saw the crowds, he had compassion on them because they were confused and helpless, like sheep without a shepherd.

– Matthew 9:36, NLT

If we knew the Word of God, believed it, and acted on it, a sick Christian should be unheard of!

"So, Jesus said to the Jews who had believed him, "If you abide in my word, you are truly my disciples, and you will know the truth, and the truth will set you free."

– John 8:31-32, ESV

Think of it this way, how can you and I be "in Christ" and filled with the Holy Spirit – yet at the same time be defenseless prey for Satan?

We were saved because we know that Christ and His Holy Spirit are more powerful than any devil. Therefore, how is Satan able to put thousands of Christians [whom Christ has freed from oppression] back into the bondage of anxiety, fear, and pain?

Brothers and Sisters, what has disabled God's protection against sickness?

Why are millions of us left to rely on prescription drugs, frequent emergency rooms in pain (paralyzed with fear), and begging for human intervention?

> *For, Who can know the LORD's thoughts? Who knows enough to teach him?" But we understand these things, for we have the mind of Christ.*
>
> – Corinthians 2:16, NLT

What happened? The Word of God says, "For God has not given us a spirit of fear, but of power and of love and of a sound mind" (2 Timothy 1:7). In the Greek translation, this tells us that we were given supernatural power, God's love, and self-control.

> **How did we lose the power of God over sickness? This is a fair question to ask of God.**

The Word of God will help us understand how we digressed to our current position of helplessness and dependence on the wisdom of man instead of the wisdom of God.

The Holy Spirit led me to painstakingly work through this dilemma in my own life.

In the Origin of Sickness section, we will discuss how God's children lost His divine power. Understanding this will enable us to regain the spiritual control that is ours and keep it!

If we dare to have faith and act on it, to believe the Word of God (exalting God's word over human intellect), we will be free of anxiety, fear, and pain!

THE ORIGIN
OF SICKNESS

*W*e must understand the true origin of sickness and how to receive the freedom (from illness) that Christ has already appropriated for us.

The Bible tells us clearly that sickness is a curse (Deuteronomy 28). It is bondage and demonic oppression (Acts 10:38).

> *And you know that God anointed Jesus of Nazareth with the Holy Spirit and with power. Then Jesus went around doing good and healing all who were oppressed by the devil, for God was with him.*
>
> – Acts 10:38, NLT

How did Satan get sickness into the earth?

Disease entered the world through the fall of Adam and Eve, but every believer who has accepted that Jesus died for his sins has already been redeemed from that curse (Galatians 3:13).

But Christ has rescued us from the curse pronounced by the law. When He was hung on the cross, He took upon Himself the curse for our wrongdoing.

For it is written in the Scriptures, "Cursed is everyone who is hung on a tree."

– Galatians 3:13, NLT

By His wounds [Jesus' beatings] we are healed (Isaiah 53:5).

In other words, healing belongs to us right now.

Christians have a blood-bought right to live free of sickness, pain, and oppression. Nonetheless, Satan goes about as a roaring lion, searching for someone he can devour (1 Peter 5:8). He is searching because He can't devour everyone. He is searching for someone to inflict fear and the pain that accompanies it.

Anxiety, fear, and pain are all tools Satan uses in his spiritual battle to reinforce the deception that keeps humans ill. God said, "My people perish for lack of knowledge" (Hosea 4:6). In other words, Christ has not only freed us from anxiety, fear, and pain, but He and His Holy Spirit guard us against Satan's continual attacks.

What can we do to be protected from satanic attacks of fear, worry, and pain? Christ is our first example.

If we look at the life of Jesus, we see that before His crucifixion, He was praying in the garden of Gethsemane. Jesus experienced great agony regarding his impending death. Yet, to be victorious in this great spiritual battle, He, too, overcame anxiety, fear, and pain.

The Bible says this:

And taking with Him Peter and the two sons of Zebedee [James and John], He began to be grieved and greatly distressed. Then He said to them, "My soul is deeply grieved so that I am almost dying of sorrow. Stay here and stay awake and keep watch with Me."

– Matthew 26:37-38, AMP

He urged the disciples to pray, saying, "The spirit is willing, but the flesh is weak."

– Matthew 26:41, NKJV

Thus, not only was Jesus facing demonic trials, but the apostles were facing danger, too.

What did Jesus know that allowed Him to proceed through this agonizing trial?

He knew the Word of God, the power of God, and most importantly – He knew God!

Jesus did not die because he had no power. He died because He submitted to death so that you and I could be healed and live! He allowed beatings by choice, not by force. By His wounds, we are healed (Isaiah 53:5).

This dangerous situation did not rob Jesus of His confident trust in His Father, God. In one discourse with the Sadducees, they questioned Jesus about marriage in the life to come.

Jesus replied, "Your mistake is that you don't know the Scriptures, and you don't know the power of God."

– Matthew 22:29, NLT

Brothers and sisters, the above scripture is profound. Stop and think about this! What we need to be healed and to stop anxiety, fear, and pain is the truth. As Christ's response (in Matthew 22:29) demonstrates, it is vital for us to know the Word of God and the power of God.

The power of God operates within us through His Holy Spirit, who indwells us and gives us new life – the very [Zoe] life of God.

And if the Spirit of Him who raised Jesus from the dead lives in you, He who raised Christ Jesus from the dead will also give life to your mortal bodies through His Spirit, who lives in you.

– Romans 8:11, AMP

BIG TAKEAWAYS

1. **ORIGIN OF SICKNESS:** God did not make us sick. It's not His fault. He doesn't want us to remain ill. As many as came to Him, Jesus healed them all. Satan is the author of sickness and disease. God said disease is a curse (Deuteronomy 28:20-68).

2. **WE CAN LIVE IN DIVINE HEALTH:** However, believers have been redeemed from the curse (Galatians 3:13), so we don't have to be sick! At the end of our life, we can fall asleep and wake up with the Lord. There is no need for us to suffer and die sick!

3. **THE REAL REASON WE ARE SICK:** The only reason we are sick today is that we haven't been taught the Word of God on divine healing. We haven't understood. God has given us spiritual tools to resist sickness.

We don't have to tolerate anxiety, fear, or pain. There is a way out.

HOW TO STOP ANXIETY & WORRY

6 KEYS TO SUCCESS

You will keep in perfect peace all who trust in you,
all whose thoughts are fixed on you!

— Isaiah 26:3, NLT

*W*orry is a cousin to fear. Like fear, it is entirely demonic. Both fear and worry support the medical condition called anxiety.

Worry is another universal plague. A great man of God once confessed that his most challenging fault was the sin of worry. So often, mothers are overly fearful about the safety of their children, and without being conscious of it, they transmit a spirit of fear and timidity directly to their children.

As a result, these children can experience delayed emotional development and stalled careers due to over-cautiousness, self-consciousness, and timidity.

> **We were raised to believe that anxiety and worry are harmless. They are very toxic to our faith life and our mental and physical health.**

So, following a lifetime of being cautious, fearful, and worried, how do we break this debilitating habit?

Jesus gave us the solution saying, "And you shall know the truth, and the truth shall make you free" (John 8:32, NKJV).

Here's the truth about anxiety and its cousin worry. Worry is a sin because God repeats in His Word, "Do not worry." Furthermore, doctors agree that prolonged fear and worry put stress on the body.

> **Uncontrolled anxiety creates pain and illness. Headaches, heart disease, and addictions are a few of the many diseases that result from ongoing stress, anxiety, and worry.**

In the Gospel of Matthew below, Jesus told us plainly that we must not worry because worry does not serve any good purpose.

IN MATTHEW 6:25-34, NKJV JESUS SAID DO NOT WORRY

"Therefore I say to you, do not worry about your life, what you will eat or what you will drink; nor about

your body, what you will put on. Is not life more than food and the body more than clothing? Look at the birds of the air, for they neither sow nor reap nor gather into barns; yet your heavenly Father feeds them. Are you not of more value than they? Which of you, by worrying can add one cubit to his stature?

"So why do you worry about clothing? Consider the lilies of the field, how they grow: they neither toil nor spin; and yet I say to you that even Solomon in all his glory was not arrayed like one of these. Now if God so clothe the grass of the field, which today is, and tomorrow is thrown into the oven, will He not much more clothe you, O you of little faith?

"Therefore do not worry, saying, 'What shall we eat?' or 'What shall we drink' or 'What shall we wear?' For after all these things the Gentiles seek. For your heavenly Father knows that you need all these things. But seek first the kingdom of God and His righteousness, and all these things shall be added to you. Therefore do not worry about tomorrow, for tomorrow will worry about its own things. Sufficient for the day is its own trouble."

– Matthew 6:25-34, NKJV

CAST YOUR CARES ON JESUS

First and foremost, we must develop unshakable faith in Jesus Christ.

In the Word of God, we are directed to give all (not some) of our worries to Christ and leave them with Him. Give all your worries and cares to God, for He cares about you (1 Peter 5:7, NLT). Cast all your anxiety on Him (NIV Translation). In this verse (1 Peter 5:7), we are given the complete answer to how to crush the sin of worry and rid ourselves of the ailment of anxiety.

We must be aware of the temptation to worry and the anxiety we feel when we have allowed fear and worry to enter our spirit. When we detect the presence of worry and its accompanying anxiety, we must consciously cast it out. We can do this through repentance [turning our hearts back to God], affirming God's promises aloud, and prayer.

OUR PRAYER TO CAST OUT FEAR, WORRY & ANXIETY

"Father God, in the Name of Jesus, I repent for worrying. Forgive me and cover me in the blood of Jesus. Father, in Hebrews 13:5, your word says that you will never leave or forsake me.

In Psalm 91:14, your word says that you will rescue me and protect me. Knowing this, I give all my concerns to you. I lift these matters in prayer to you, and I trust you to resolve them. As your word said, I do not lean on my own understanding, but I acknowledge you and trust you to direct my path in all my ways.

My Father, I will listen to you and act in obedience to your word. Right now, I take my authority to cast out every evil force.

In the powerful Name of Jesus, I command fear,
doubt, unbelief, worry, anxiety, stress, tension,
panic, and every evil spirit to leave my body
and soul immediately!

My dear Father, I thank you! I still my
emotions and see the glory of the LORD! Amen.
Thank you, Jesus!"

As part of our prayer, it is perfectly acceptable to ask God for specific requests. In fact, God delights in specific requests because this builds our faith and confirms His intervention.

God often blesses us with much more than we asked for. He may direct us to raise our standards, to wait, or to proceed in another direction. God is so wonderful!

Through repetition, we consistently refuse anxiety, worry, depression, and all other negative emotions. We consciously resist and reject anxiety through our awareness of its presence, affirmations, prayers, and trust in God. As a result of our refusal to be anxious, we automatically starve anxiety to death!

> **The Holy Spirit empowers believers to control anxiety and stress without drugs if we are willing to act on the Word of God.**

Three powerful keys to success in this area are 1) daily expressions of praise and gratitude toward Christ and thinking on good things, 2) audibly reciting the promises of God, and 3) in the name of Jesus, audibly commanding the spirit of fear or specific pains to leave our bodies instantly.

*The young women will dance for joy, and
the men—old and young—will join in the
celebration. I will turn their mourning into joy.
I will comfort them and exchange their sorrow
for rejoicing.*

– Jeremiah 31:13, NLT

*Fear not, for I am with you; Be not dismayed,
for I am your God. I will strengthen you,
Yes, I will help you, I will uphold you with
My righteous right hand.*

– Isaiah 41:10, NKJV

---

6 STEPS TO CRUSH ANXIETY (BASED ON PHILIPPIANS 4:16)

*Don't worry about anything; instead, pray
about everything. Tell God what you need,
and thank him for all he has done.*

– Philippians 4:16, NLT

Based on Philippians 4:16, do this:

1. Decide not to worry about anything! Worry is useless and a waste of your energy.

2. Pray and hand over the entire matter to God. Then, let it go! Trust Him. Tell God exactly what you want and need.

3. Thank God (in advance) for hearing your prayer and helping you.

4. Memorize Psalm 91. (I did it! It was fun).

5. Stop judging yourself, circumstances, and others! Instead, fix your thoughts on good things.

6. Memorize the below two scriptures. Say them aloud all day, meditate on them, and say them to yourself as you drift off to a peaceful sleep.

You will keep in perfect peace all who trust in you, all whose thoughts are fixed on you!

— Isaiah 26:3, NLT

Finally, brethren, whatever things are true, whatever things are noble, whatever things are just, whatever things are pure, whatever things are lovely, whatever things are of good report, if there is any virtue and if there is anything praiseworthy— meditate on these things.

— Philippians 4:8, NKJV

The key to crushing anxiety and worry is to stop judging yourself, your circumstances, and others. Then, deliberately fix your thoughts on Jesus, The Lord Who Heals us. Meditate on the Word of God and good news.

....casting all your cares [all your anxieties, all your worries, and all your concerns, once and for all] on

Him, for He cares about you [with deepest affection, and watches over you very carefully].

– 1 Peter 5:7, AMP

The LORD will give strength to His people; The LORD will bless His people with peace.

– Psalm 29:11, NKJV

HOW TO STOP FEAR

IN 3 STEPS

For God has not given us a spirit of fear and timidity,
but of power, love, and self-discipline.

– 2 Timothy 1:7, NLT

Look, I have given you authority over all the power
of the enemy, and you can walk among snakes and
scorpions and crush them. Nothing will injure you.

– Luke 10:19, NLT

Never forget that fear is demonic. The Word of
God tells us that God did not give us a spirit of fear.

*F*ear is that threatening inner voice that invades our thoughts to shatter our faith in the Word of God. Jesus was fearless.

"Don't be afraid of those who want to kill your body;
they cannot touch your soul. Fear only God, who can
destroy both soul and body in hell.

– Matthew 10:28, NLT

The apostle Paul said, "For God hath not given us a spirit of fear; but of power, and of love, and a sound mind" (2 Timothy 1:7, KJB). In other words, fear is a spirit, but it is an ungodly spirit.

God wants us to know He has already given us the power to conquer fear through our confidence in His protective love and the soundness of mind that comes from knowing His word.

"There is no fear in love, but perfect love casteth out fear: because fear hath torment. He that feareth is not made perfect in love."

– 1 John 4:18, KJB

The spirit of fear torments its victims with emotional and sometimes unrelenting physical pain. Therefore, anyone who suffers from pain must resist the spirit of fear.

Knowing that fear is demonic helps us become more aware of its presence and resist and cancel it. Thus, both worry and anxiety are closely related to fear.

The spirit of fear is a spirit of bondage. "For you did not receive the spirit of bondage again to fear, but you received the Spirit of adoption by whom we cry 'Abba Father'" (Romans 8:15, NKJV). Speaking of the death and resurrection of Christ, the writer of Hebrews says, "Only in this way, could He set free all who have lived their lives as slaves to the fear of dying" (Hebrews 2:15, NLT).

The spirit of fear lies and deceives its victims. Fear often has its victims cringing over a future event that has not occurred and will never occur.

Fear launches thoughts, feelings, and inner words of impending doom that open the door to the same circumstance or event that is dreaded. In the book of Job, he said,

"For the thing, I greatly feared has come upon me, And what I dreaded has happened to me" (Job 3:25, NKJV).

———————

Here's what fear does to those who don't resist it.

1. Fear pollutes our faith.

2. Fear puts us in bondage (Romans 8:15). Fear brings torment. Fear often causes the onset and escalation of physical pain or other symptoms of illness.

3. Fear paralyzes us so that we can't move ahead or excel.

4. Fear deceives us and clouds the mind into making poor decisions.

5. Fear can lead to sin against God and others through our desperation.

6. Fear opens the door for other forces of evil such as unbelief, doubt, worry, anxiety, depression, panic, and other influences and symptoms.

> **Anyone who wishes to walk in divine health must resist every form of fear.**

We must resist the fear of death, the fear of sickness, and the fear of worsening illness. Resist the fear of doctors, medications, operations, and the fear of foods. Turn away from the fear of people and the fear of upcoming circumstances. All these fears and any other fear must be resisted. We resist by meditating on Christ and the biblical promises of God.

> **Fear is a *lying* spirit commonly known as "false evidence appearing real."**

Therefore, submit to God. Resist the devil, and he will flee from you.

– James 4:7, NKJV

Jesus said, "Look, I have given you authority over all the power of the enemy, and you can walk among snakes and scorpions and crush them. Nothing will injure you."

– Luke 10:19, NLT

> **Every believer should know Luke 10:19 by heart!**

The New Living Translation says, "For God has not given us a spirit of fear and timidity [cowardice], but of power, love, and self-discipline" (2 Timothy 1:7, NLT).

This scripture holds three vital keys to be set free from the bondage of fear.

OUR GOD-GIVEN POWER

See Luke 10:19 above. We must know our God-given power. Satan has no power over us unless we give it to him through lack of knowledge, fear, unbelief, or sin. We can command demons, sickness, and pain to leave our bodies in the Name of Jesus. Jesus said, "Heal the sick, raise the dead, cure those with leprosy, and cast out demons. Give as freely as you have received!" (Matthew 10:8, NLT).

LOVE NEVER FAILS

Meditate on God's love toward us personally. We must live with the revelation of how much God loves us to feel confident in His protection and return His love.

Make a list of all the reasons you know God loves you personally. Throughout your life, what has He done for you? Have you seen or experienced His miracles? Write them down.

No power in the sky above or in the earth below—
indeed, nothing in all creation will ever be able to
separate us from the love of God that is revealed in
Christ Jesus our Lord.

– Romans 8:39, NLT

Ask God in prayer to give you the revelation of His love for you.

Trusting in God's love for us helps to release miracles when we need them.

Additionally, we must walk in love with others.

A SOUND MIND AND SELF-DISCIPLINE

Our responses and decisions are all dictated by what we know and believe. A sound mind is a result of knowing the truth.

Observing random sensory evidence does not always reveal the truth. Likewise, as a result of the sound mind and self-discipline, we are empowered (through knowledge of the truth) to resist fear, worry, and its tormenting pain.

"And you shall know the truth, and the truth shall
make you free."

– John 8:32, NKJV

To crush fear, we must recognize it, resist it, and cast it down in favor of believing and speaking the Word of

God. We don't have to memorize the entire Bible, but we should know foundational scriptures that crush fear.

One favorite scripture is, "Even though I walk through the darkest valley, I will fear no evil, for you are with me; your rod and your staff, they comfort me" (Psalm 23:4, NIV).

When fear rears its ugly head, we must know instantly that there is nothing to fear because God is always with us! He is the one who is protecting us.

Amid the COVID-19 pandemic, by law, citizens wore masks and gloves and we practiced social distancing – but God alone has saved each of our lives.

Here are additional practices to crush fear and worry.

SPEAK THE WORD - NOT YOUR CIRCUMSTANCES!

Our first defense against fear is knowing, thinking, and speaking the Word of God. We could say inwardly or audibly, "I fear no evil for God is with me" (Psalm 23:4). Or we could say, "Nothing by any means can harm me" (Luke 10:19).

> **When Jesus Christ was tempted by Satan in the wilderness, He resisted the devil by quoting the Word of God directly to the devil (Matthew 4:4-11). As a result, Satan left!**

When fearful thoughts arise, we must meditate on the Word of God only. We are attacked through our minds. God uses our minds to direct us and Satan attempts to twist our minds to destroy us.

Therefore, we cannot allow fearful thoughts to persist. They must be cast out by overriding them with the Word of God.

What we are thinking and what we believe will eventually come out of our mouths.

Divine healing can be prevented when we are inconsistent and out of alignment.

If we quote the word, "By His stripes, I was healed," we can nullify our testimony if simultaneously, we are telling others we are still sick.

Honestly, we can tell a doctor our symptoms without agreeing that we have a disease and spreading that among family members. How can we be sick and well at the same time?

> When I was battling illness, during my prayer time, Christ said this to me, "SEE YOURSELF WELL!" We must see what we believe we can achieve.

Our own bodies will stay in alignment with what we honestly believe and repeat.

FEARLESSLY, CAST OUT DEMONS IN THE NAME OF JESUS.

Jesus told us to cast out demons (Matthew 10:8).

We can say, "In the Name of Jesus, spirit of fear, I command you to leave!" Expect it to obey you. Exalt the Word of God over all sense knowledge. Continue to meditate on and/or recite the promises of God until your peace is completely restored.

You will keep him in perfect peace, Whose mind is stayed on You Because he trusts in You.

– Isaiah 26:3 NKJV

THINK ABOUT GOOD THINGS

Finally, brothers, whatever is true, whatever is honorable, whatever is just, whatever is pure, whatever is lovely, whatever is commendable, if there is any excellence, if there is anything worthy of praise, think about these things.

– Philippians 4:8, ESV

HOW TO STOP FEAR IN 3 STEPS:

1. Remember, fear is satanic. God did not give you a spirit of fear (2 Timothy 1:7). So, resist fear, and it will flee.

2. If fear tries to seize you, speak the Word of God aloud. Say, "Nothing by any means shall harm me!" (Luke 10:19). Then, change your thoughts immediately and think about good things (Philippians 4:8).

3. During an attack of fear, try to stop the habit of involving others. Remember, God is always with you. Recite Psalm 91 and meditate on every sentence. You may calm down and drift off to a peaceful nap.

If you practice these three steps, you will find that you have begun to stop having attacks of any kind.

HOW TO STOP PHYSICAL PAIN

IN 7 STEPS

For God has not given us a spirit of cowardice, but of power, and of love, and of self-control.

– 2 Timothy 1:7, BLB

*A*s you recall, the Word of God tells us that fear has torment (1 John 4:18).

Torment often manifests as physical pain. The antidote to pain is the exact antidote that we used for anxiety and fear. Jesus gave us the solution saying, "And you shall know the truth, and the truth shall make you free" (John 8:32, NKJV).

The truth is that Jesus has already conquered every source of pain. He has defeated Satan and sin through His death on the cross. Christ has made us righteous before God.

> **No devil has a legal right to afflict a born-again believer with pain and sickness.**

Our pain was put on Jesus as He hung on the cross. Christ gave us the power to cast out the spirit of infirmity, disease, and its resulting pain. The Bible tells us that the current state of every new believer is divine health. Pain and sickness have been put away.

See Matthew 8:17 below.

When evening came, many who were demon-possessed were brought to him, and he drove out the spirits with a word and healed all the sick. This was to fulfill what was spoken through the prophet Isaiah: "He took up our infirmities and bore our diseases."

– Matthew 8:16-17, NIV

It is vital to realize that we must embrace the boldness that comes from knowing that through Christ, we are in right standing with God. How do we know that we are in the faith?

Our faith is confirmed by our actions.

"Faith without work is dead."

– James 2:20, KJB

We agree that we are healed through our new birth in Christ – right now, and our healing is received through faith. The manifestation of healing in our bodies can be instant or gradual.

However, if we never act on the knowledge of our righteousness and freedom from sickness, this denial of our power can prevent us from receiving our healing.

Unfortunately, many Christians have been gradually brainwashed to believe in the power of sickness as superior to the power of God.

A mindset of unbelief absolutely prevents Jesus Christ and the Holy Spirit from healing our bodies. The failure to act and our sin consciousness pollute the faith that is necessary for the manifestation of bodily healing.

Often, the pain has been tolerated for months or years. Jesus may remove it through one miracle, or it may diminish gradually as we read the Word of God and learn to use our spiritual authority.

Spiritual authority is the practice of strategically and consistently boldly acting on God's word. To succeed in crushing pain, we must learn to exalt the Word of God over the five senses and sense realm.

So we don't look at the troubles we can see now;
rather, we fix our gaze on things that cannot be seen.
For the things we see now will soon be gone, but the
things we cannot see will last forever.
                                        – 2 Corinthians 4:18, NLT

When we understand that we are well right now, it begs the question, "Why am I experiencing pain and symptoms?" We experience pain and symptoms because we have not understood how to receive from God, nor have we consistently sought God for the answer.

God works through our minds, and so does the enemy. To change our reality, first, God changes our thinking. He often must clear away fear, doubt, unbelief, unforgiveness, and negativity.

Most importantly, He must give us the confidence to act on what we believe.

> **Pain is closely related to the spirit of fear. Fear escalates pain and other symptoms.**

If we resist fear and worry, pain (and many sicknesses) begin to diminish or disappear altogether.

––––––––––

Below are seven ways to partner with the Holy Spirit to achieve freedom from pain and any sickness or demonic oppression.

7-PART SYSTEM TO CRUSH PAIN

1. **HAVE FAITH IN GOD** – Jesus is our healer. Trust in His love and faithfulness toward us. Most importantly, we must fellowship with God daily. Our confidence in His love and faithfulness skyrockets when we know Him intimately through daily prayer and Bible study.

   Each time we meet someone who manifests the undeniable power of God, it comes as no surprise to learn how much consistent time they have spent daily alone in the presence of God.

2. **FAITH IN THE WORD OF GOD** – Have unshakable faith in the healing scriptures. We should meditate on them and speak them daily over our bodies. Refuse to think or speak contrary to the Word of God.

3. **PRAISE GOD FOR THE VICTORY** – Great faith is released when we begin to see ourselves well and praise Him for His faithfulness. We must praise God for His faithfulness and rescue even in the face of symptoms.

4. **BOLDLY COMMAND PAIN TO LEAVE** – Jesus commissioned us to heal the sick and cast out demons. In full authority, say to your body, "In the Name of Jesus, I rebuke fear, pain, and any spirit of infirmity in my body. In Jesus' Name, I command you to leave my body now – and never return!"

Expect it to leave. The Name of Jesus has great power, and it is crucial for us to openly and audibly refuse to allow any demonic presence to oppress us.

5. **FOCUS ON THE WORD & HEALING SCRIPTURES** – To remove pain, we must stop fear, worrying, and thinking about depressing things. Sometimes, we must stop watching too much of the daily news.

Avoid meditating on sickness, pain, defeat, and other negative thoughts. This is very important. Ongoing healing requires maintaining a peaceful, stress-free, and positive mindset.

6. **ACT TO CRUSH PAIN** – The Bible says faith without action is dead (James 2:20). God is keeping us alive so that our victorious lives will give Him glory and bless others.

Begin to do things to bless yourself and others you previously put off (because of illness). Create an atmosphere of joy in your life that comes from living up to your full potential.

Ask the Holy Spirit to show you how to act on your faith that you already have your healing. Begin to do all the healthy things that you should be doing!

7. **FAITH WORKS BY LOVE** – Close the door to Satan! Love is the greatest commandment. Thousands of

people are very sick because they have chosen to hold anger, disappointment, resentment, unforgiveness, and rage in their hearts.

Our bodies were not created to house any negative emotions. Anger and resentment are poison. One great man of God said he would avoid unforgiveness just as he would avoid a rattlesnake.

To avoid anxiety, fear, and pain, we must forgive ourselves and forgive anyone who has hurt or harmed us.

To hold on to unforgiveness is to cling to evil.

Clinging to sin dilutes or completely destroys our faith and confidence in God.

FREELY FORGIVE!

Say this prayer, "Father God, I come to you just as I am. I believe that Jesus Christ is the Son of God. He died for my sins and rose again. Father, in the Name of Jesus, I ask that you forgive all my sins, especially the sin of unforgiveness.

I forgive everyone who has hurt, harmed, and wronged me. I ask you to forgive them, too, because you have been merciful toward me. Help me cleanse my heart of all hidden resentments.

Father, I thank you that right now, I am saved and forgiven. Lord Jesus, come into my life and fill me with your precious Holy Spirit. Live your life in and through me. Jesus, from this day forward, I belong to You.

Lord, I receive your healing virtue that has removed all anxiety, fear, sickness, and pain. Thank you for drenching my mind and heart with your love. In Jesus' Name, Amen."

SUMMARY

As shared above, practicing *unconditional love* toward others will bring an immense amount of joy, peace, and inner calm into our lives. However, if we face any health challenge, we must be prepared to succeed in any spiritual battle.

> **It occurred to me that one reason we have incurable diseases today is that most doctors are not trained to remove the demons that are oppressing patients.**

Our wonderful doctors can prescribe medications to calm the symptoms or stop the pain, but if the root is demonic oppression, it may be labeled *incurable*.

What is wonderful about Jesus, the Lord our Healer, is that no condition is *incurable* with Jesus. Conditions are only *incurable* according to the earthly sciences. Utilizing the word and wisdom of God, *nothing* is incurable!

Therefore, put on every piece of God's armor so you will be able to resist the enemy in the time of evil. Then after the battle you will still be standing firm.

– Ephesians 6:13, NLT

5 TIPS TO HALT PAIN

1. **BE SPIRITUALLY MINDED:** Let your spirit control your mind by meditating on Jesus and His word. This calming of the soul will help prevent bouts of pain.

Write down scriptures that overcome pain and quote them all day and as you fall asleep. Nothing is as powerful as the Word of God.

2. **BE PRUDENT:** Naturally speaking, take better care of yourself. Instead of relying on drugs to survive the day, eat better, drink sufficient water, and get more sleep.

3. **AVOID ANGER AND STRIFE:** Avoid all strife, as strife can create tension in the body, translating to pain.

4. **CAST OUT DEMONS:** Cast out the spirit of infirmity. Say aloud, "In the Name of Jesus, spirits of pain, sickness, disease, and infirmity, I command you to leave my body now!" Say it once - but firmly. Expect the pain to leave. If you use the authority Jesus gave you, you will be amazed at how many times your pains just vanish! There is power in the Name of Jesus. As you begin to practice walking in the spirit, speaking the Word of God, controlling your thoughts, and taking better care of yourself, your health will *drastically* improve.

5. **COMMAND YOUR BODY TO BE REBUILT:** Say aloud, "In the Name of Jesus, body, I command you to be rebuilt, restored, and repaired. Function in the perfection of Jesus. I have been redeemed from the curse" (Galatians 3:13). Have faith that you received a new body part or a new organ when you spoke.

For we live by faith, not by sight.

– 2 Corinthians 5:7, NIV

STOP RECURRING ATTACKS

REFUSE TO BE MOVED
OR DECEIVED

But don't rejoice because evil spirits obey you; rejoice because your names are registered in heaven.

– Luke 10:20, NLT

*B*elievers no longer have a reason to fear death. Jesus said, "I am he that liveth, and was dead; and, behold, I am alive for evermore, Amen; and have the keys of hell and of death" (Revelation 1:18, KJB).

Thus, Jesus has taken the keys to hell and death.

> **Satan no longer has any power to end the life of a believer who is in Christ.**

*Because God's children are human beings—made of flesh and blood—the Son also became flesh and blood. For only as a human being could he die, and only by dying **could he break the power of the devil, who had the power of death.** Only in this way could he set free all who have lived their lives as slaves to the fear of dying.*

— Hebrews 2:14-15, NLT

And I give them eternal life, and they shall never perish; neither shall anyone snatch them out of My hand.

— John 10:28, NKJV

When symptoms of illness strike our bodies, we can relax in John 10:28, knowing that no one can take us from Jesus! Jesus alone has the keys to death. We are safe in His care.

> **Satan will use every sensory evidence that he can summon to move us from faith to fear.**

To gain mastery over recurring attacks, we must refuse to exalt sensory evidence over the Word of God. The Word of God directly contradicts sensory facts. God's Word is truth, and truth has the power to alter facts.

For instance, it may be a fact that you have no money in your purse, but the truth may be that you have a thousand dollars in the bank.

God's Word spoken in faith overrides and changes sensory facts. It is a fact that Satan is on the rampage, but the truth is that he has already been utterly defeated by Jesus.

We demolish arguments and every pretension that sets itself up against the knowledge of God, and we take captive every thought to make it obedient to Christ.

– 2 Corinthians 10:5, NIV

3 REASONS FOR RECURRING ATTACKS

1. **Lack of Knowledge** - We must speak the Word of God to stop an attack. If we resist the devil (with the Word), he will flee (James 4:7). Anxiety, fear, and pain can all be stopped by speaking the Word of God. We must memorize our healing scriptures and know the Word of God concerning divine healing.

2. **Believing Lies** - During attacks, if we don't stand on God's Word by speaking it out loud and over our bodies, we will begin to focus on sensory evidence such as evil reports, symptoms, and what the spirit of fear is saying.

3. **Allowing Fear to Oppress Us** - Attacks are often characterized by an evil spirit of fear which brings torment. Torment manifests as pain.

If we don't tell the spirits of fear, infirmity, and pain to leave in the Name of Jesus, we might become overwhelmed by circumstances. Unfortunately, few Christians have been taught to send the devil, fear, and pain packing. We can bind (stop) anxiety, fear, and pain.

"I tell you the truth, whatever you forbid on earth will be forbidden in heaven, and whatever you permit on earth will be permitted in heaven."

– Matthew 18:18, NLT

"Assuredly, I say to you, whatever you bind on earth will be bound in heaven, and whatever you loose on earth will be loosed in heaven."

– Matthew 18:18, NKJV

HOW TO STOP RECURRING ATTACKS

1. **Confess God's Word Daily** - Believers who have gained mastery over anxiety, fear, and pain have done so because they speak the Word of God over their bodies daily. Satan cannot overcome us if we know the Word of God, believe it, and *enforce it.*

2. **Stop Contradicting the Word of God** - The Word of God says, "By His stripes, you were healed." That means when Jesus died on the cross, you were healed and set from sin and infirmity. Meditate on Isaiah 53:4-5 and Matthew 8:17.

If we want anxiety, fear, and pain to stop attacking us, we must stop telling others that we are sick. Is that lying? No. On a spiritual level, we can be well yet experience symptoms on the natural level. The prophet Jonah called these "lying vanities" (Jonah 2:8).

If we truly believe the Word of God, we know that we are not ill.

Our symptoms are a fact, but they are not the truth.

The Word of God is the truth. In the following scripture, God tells us plainly that when God's Word is spoken, it changes our circumstances.

So shall My word be that goes forth from My mouth; It shall not return to Me void, But it shall accomplish what I please, And it shall prosper in the thing for which I sent it.

– Isaiah 55:11, NKJV

We must pay attention to what we are saying. We can't ask God to heal us and confess (in the Name of Jesus) that we are healed and then tell everyone we know that we have diseases.

If we want to get well and stay well, we must repeatedly tell our bodies the truth, which is, "By Jesus' stripes, I was healed."

Our bodies are reacting to what we are saying. If we speak death, the body begins to die. If we speak life, the body begins to repair itself. Our bodies hear and believe everything we are saying.

The Bible says it this way, "Death and life are in the power of the tongue, And those who love it will eat its fruit."

– Proverbs 18:21, NKJV

This means that daily, we are speaking our destinies without knowing it.

3. **Stop Agreeing with Evil Reports** – If we want to stop fear, anxiety, and pain, we must stop agreeing and receiving any news that we are sick.

If we are standing on the Word of God and a professional tells us we have a disease, we can move forward with treatment without verbally agreeing that we have a condition. Professionals don't ask us. They tell us.

Despite sensory evidence of sickness, we must speak the Word of God over the situation and stand on the Word of God. If anyone asks how we are doing, we must tell the truth and say, "The doctor said this, but I know I will be fine."

We must believe the Word of God and speak confidently to everyone about our healing. Our bodies hear us and will respond with wellness!

Jesus said, speak to your mountain and tell it to move!

Jesus shared this powerful principle with His disciples when he said this.

So Jesus answered and said to them, "Assuredly, I say to you, if you have faith and do not doubt, you will not only do what was done to the fig tree but also if you say to this mountain, 'Be removed and be cast

*into the sea,' it will be done. And whatever things you
ask in prayer, believing, you will receive."*

– Matthew 21:21-22, NKJV

Remember that Jesus has given us authority and power
to use His name to overturn all the work of the enemy!

*Look, I have given you authority over all the power
of the enemy, and you can walk among snakes and
scorpions and crush them. Nothing will injure you.*

– Luke 10:19, NLT

*"And in that day you will ask Me nothing. Most
assuredly, I say to you, whatever you ask the Father
in My name He will give you."*

– John 16:23, NKJV

Stand on the Word of God. Consistently, speak the Word of
God over your body. You will experience miracles!

HOW TO PRAY FOR OUR LOVED ONES

*T*he Word of God tells us clearly that we should pray for the health of others. We are given many different ways to do this.

> *Is anyone among you sick? Let them call the elders of the church to pray over them and anoint them with oil in the name of the Lord. And the prayer offered in faith will make the sick person well; the Lord will raise them up. If they have sinned, they will be forgiven.*
> — James 5:14-15, NIV

> *Therefore, confess your sins to one another and pray for one another, so that you may be healed. The prayer of a righteous person is very powerful in its effect.*
> — James 5:16, CSB

Below are four ways we can pray for others.

1. We can pray for others up close or at a distance.

2. Up close, we can lay hands on others and anoint them with oil.

3. We can agree with them (or with others) in prayer.

4. We can speak directly to their body and command their body to be healed in the Name of Jesus.

Please note that we do not have to be super saints, ministers, or elders to pray for others. Christ has given all Christians this charge to pray for one another.

I also tell you this: If two of you agree here on earth concerning anything you ask, my Father in heaven will do it for you.

– Matthew 18:19, NLT

Psalm 91 is a great prayer to say for ourselves, our families, and for others.

Up close or at a distance we can pray for others.

We can pray the following:

"Father, I touch and agree with Mary asking you to keep her healed and well. We know that by Jesus' stripes, Mary was healed. We thank you for covering her in the blood of Jesus and helping her quickly manifest her joints' healing. We ask this in the Name of Jesus and believe that we have received it. Thank you, Jesus! Amen."

Up close or at a distance, we can speak directly to their body.

We can say this:

"Body of Mary Smith (Ethel's Daughter), I am speaking to you. In the Name of Jesus, I command every illness, sickness, disease trying to invade your body to die at the root. I command every pain, every ache, every evil spirit to leave you - now! Body of Mary Smith, be rebuilt and repaired now - function in perfection. Mary Smith shall not die but live and give glory to God. In the Name of Jesus, I call it done! Thank you, Jesus!"

As you pray for yourself and others, always speak boldly and have confidence in your prayers.

All that is required to pray for others is our own faith. Remember, in James 5:14-15, we are told that our prayer in faith will heal the sick.

It works for those who believe it!

SEVEN KEYS TO VICTORY

WE HAVE ARMOR & PROTECTION

*W*e know that we are saved and have God's Spirit. With that in mind, what practical steps should we take to remove fear, worry, and pain? Based on the Word of God, in response to attacks of anxiety, fear, and pain, here's what we must know and do.

> *Jesus responded, "Why are you afraid? You have so little faith!" Then he got up and rebuked the wind and waves, and suddenly there was a great calm.*
>
> – Matthew 8:26, NLT

1. **SPEAK THE WORD OF GOD** – The Word of God and the Name of Jesus are two of the most powerful weapons on earth. The Word and God Himself are one and the same (John 1:1). The Word is sharper than a

sword and divides between soul and spirit, joints and marrow (Hebrews 4:12).

> There is no name (of any illness) that has power over the name of Jesus when it is used in faith (Philippians 2:9).

2. **THINK ON GOOD THINGS** – Fear, worry, and pain are thwarted when we meditate on (and recite) the Word of God instead of our symptoms. Whatever is true, lovely, and praiseworthy is what we must think (Philippians 4:8).

3. **ATTACKS OF FEAR (& PANIC) ARE DEMONIC** – Know with certainty that fear is a demonic spirit. It attracts the very thing we fear (2 Timothy 1:7; Job 3:25). Jesus said, do not worry (Matthew 6:25). Never, ever worry! He said, "Come to Me, and I will give you rest" (Matthew 11:28). You are fighting for your faith (1 Timothy 6:12).

4. **FEAR ESCALATES PHYSICAL PAIN** – Fear has torment (1 John 4:8). Both physical and emotional pain can escalate (and get much worse) in the presence of fear and worry.

5. **RESIST** – We must resist fear (James 4:7). We resist by reciting the Word of God, as Christ did (Matthew 4:4). During attacks of fear or anxiety, we must say aloud, "For God has not given me a spirit of fear, but of power and of love and of a sound mind" (2 Timothy 1:7, NKJV).

6. **REST IN CHRIST'S LOVE AND FAITHFULNESS** – Love casts out fear (1 John 4:8). When we are confident of God's loving presence, we can relax. God's people were reminded, "And the LORD, He is the One

who goes before you. He will be with you, He will not leave you nor forsake you; do not fear nor be dismayed" (Deuteronomy 31:8). God is faithful. He will never leave us or let us down.

7. **TAKE ACTION** – Believing is not enough. We must take action by speaking His healing scriptures over our bodies and affirming our faith to anyone we talk to. Know that by Jesus' stripes, we were already healed (1 Peter 2:24). We must trust in what God's Holy Spirit tells you to do in the moment, not in what fear tells you to do.

8. When Jesus was tempted by Satan, He said, "It is written," and He quoted the direct Word of God (Matthew 4:4) to overcome Satan's attacks. Jesus did not obey what Satan was urging Him to do. Instead, He acted according to what the Holy Spirit was leading Him to do. As a result, God was faithful, and Jesus was comforted (Matthew 4:11).

How does this work in our everyday circumstances?

MY PERSONAL EXPERIENCE

I used to be seized with fear concerning physical attacks of sickness.

> I would call those closest to me to put them on alarm and often run to the hospital emergency room for help. It was fear, doubt, worry, and pain that kept me running back and forth.

59

During one visit to the emergency room, a kind female doctor gave me a tip. She told me that my alarm (constant fear and worry) was making my symptoms worse!

This was a medical doctor telling me what Jesus said over two thousand years ago, "Do not worry (Matthew 6:31)."

We take the Lord's command (to stop worrying) for granted, but doctors have long warned patients that (the ongoing stress of) worrying is a precursor to disease and premature death.

Over the next few months, I began to meditate more deeply on the Word of God and release faith in the healing promises of God.

Once I began to truly believe the healing promises of God, I was greatly relieved of the alarm, painful torment, and burdens I had placed on myself and our family.

I knew that Christ and His Spirit were within me, and (according to God's Word) I am healed right now (Isaiah 53:5).

> **If not resisted, the demonic spirit of fear will wreak havoc on us. I found that the more I acted on the Word of God instead of acting in fear, the more physical relief I enjoyed.**

As we examine the scriptures, we see other men and women of God intimately acquainted with the Lord, firmly trusting in His promises and His power.

WHY WE DON'T HAVE TO BE ANXIOUS OR FEARFUL

The prophet Daniel was rescued from the lion's den because he knew the power of God (Daniel 6). So likewise, the three Hebrew boys were rescued from a fiery furnace because they knew the power of God (Daniel 3:6). It was their faith in God, their faith in the promises of God, and the power of God that shielded them from the fear, worry, and pain that threatened their lives.

Christ lives in us, and we are the temple (dwelling place) of His Holy Spirit. When it comes to divine healing, it is our life in Christ and the power of the Holy Spirit that release miracles of healing restoration to every organ and cell of our bodies.

Speaking to the church, Paul says, "Or do you not know that your body is the temple of the Holy Spirit who is in you, whom you have from God, and you are not your own?"

– 1 Corinthians 6:19, NKJV

If we desire complete wellness, we must turn from exalting man's wisdom over the wisdom of God.

Jesus Christ lives in us with His Holy Spirit to protect us and guide us. God said, "For he will rescue you from every trap and protect you from deadly disease."

– Psalm 91:3, NLT

Most importantly, God told us exactly what we must do to qualify for His protection.

The LORD says, "I will rescue those who love me. I will protect those who trust in my name. When they call

on me, I will answer; I will be with them in trouble.
I will rescue and honor them. I will reward them with
long life and give them my salvation."

– Psalm 91:14-16, NLT

My son, pay attention to my words and be willing to
learn; Open your ears to my sayings. Do not let them
escape from your sight; Keep them in the center of
your heart. For they are life to those who find them,
And healing and health to all their flesh.

– Proverbs 4:20-22, AMP

Therefore say to them, 'Thus says the LORD of hosts:
"Return to Me," says the LORD of hosts, "and I will
return to you," says the LORD of hosts.

– Zechariah 1:3, NKJV

Crushing anxiety, fear, and pain is a spiritual battle.

It is the Lord's battle, and He has promised His people He would fight for them. However, throughout His Word, He encouraged us to love Him, trust in Him, and listen to Him. This means believing and acting on His healing promises.

The Holy Spirit has been placed within each of us to crush the fear, worry, and pain that wishes to trap us within the bondage of sickness.

Jesus set us free!

And deliver them who through fear of death were all
their lifetime subject to bondage.

– Hebrews 2:15, KJB

ACKNOWLEDGE THE HOLY SPIRIT

*L*ike our Father God and Jesus, the Holy Spirit is a person within the Godhead who loves us deeply. He lives within every believer and yearns to be acknowledged by us.

As we communicate with Him daily, He infuses us with the power of Almighty God. The Holy Spirit empowers us to crush anxiety, fear, and pain.

WHAT WE MUST KNOW ABOUT THE HOLY SPIRIT

The Holy Spirit is a person.

God is a Trinity. He is the Father, Son, and Holy Spirit. The Holy Spirit is God's own Spirit; therefore, He knows the mind of Almighty God.

The Holy Spirit is a person with His own distinct personality.

We should cultivate a personal relationship with the Holy Spirit.

Just as we have a relationship directly with our Father, God, and with Jesus, we should have a close, intimate relationship with the Holy Spirit.

We should love Him, communicate directly with Him, and acknowledge Him daily. We should ask for His help, thank Him, worship Him, and show affection toward Him.

> *May the grace of the Lord Jesus Christ, the love of God, and the fellowship of the Holy Spirit be with you all.*
> – 2 Corinthians 13:14, NLT

Saved and baptized believers automatically receive the gift of the Holy Spirit. He lives inside of us.

> *Then Peter said to them, "Repent, and let every one of you be baptized in the name of Jesus Christ for the remission of sins; and you shall receive the gift of the Holy Spirit."*
> – Acts 2:38, NKJV

> *Do you not know that you are the temple of God and that the Spirit of God dwells in you?*
> – 1 Corinthians 3:16, NKJV

The Holy Spirit helps us and will be with us forever. He frees us from all bondage. He gives us power and self-control.

It is the Holy Spirit who changes our hearts after we are saved. We have the love of God and His godly attributes.

And this hope will not lead to disappointment. For we know how dearly God loves us because he has given us the Holy Spirit to fill our hearts with his love.

- Romans 5:5, NLT

But the Holy Spirit produces this kind of fruit in our lives: love, joy, peace, patience, kindness, goodness, faithfulness, gentleness, and self-control. There is no law against these things!

– Galatians 5:22-23, NLT

For God has not given us a spirit of fear and timidity, but of power, love, and self-discipline.

– 2 Timothy 1:7, NLT

The Holy Spirit infuses us with the power of God.

But you will receive power when the Holy Spirit comes upon you. And you will be my witnesses, telling people about me everywhere—in Jerusalem, throughout Judea, in Samaria, and to the ends of the earth.

– Acts 1:8, NLT

God said that in these last days, He would generously give His Spirit to believers. We see this manifesting today.

'In the last days,' God says, 'I will pour out my Spirit upon all people. Your sons and daughters will prophesy. Your young men will see visions, and your old men will dream dreams. In those days I will pour out my Spirit even on my servants—men and women alike— and they will prophesy.'

– Acts 2:17-18, NLT

God's Holy Spirit loves us dearly and He yearns to hear from us and to talk to us. The Bible says He is our Comforter and our Counselor. So read as many books as you can about the Holy Spirit and begin to strengthen your relationship with Him.

> *And I will ask the Father, and He will give you another Helper (Comforter, Advocate, Intercessor— Counselor, Strengthener, Standby), to be with you forever ...*
>
> – John 14:16, AMP

7 REASONS GOD FILLS US WITH HIS HOLY SPIRIT

As a believer, it is essential that we understand the ministry of the Holy Spirit and His importance. Here are seven (7) of the reasons that we must be filled with the Holy Spirit.

1. SALVATION

2. LIFE

3. HOLINESS

4. PRAYER

5. TRUTH

6. POWER

7. MIRACLES

THE OFFICE OF THE HOLY SPIRIT

Throughout the Bible, numerous scriptures tell us who the Holy Spirit is and what He does for believers. Read the following explanations of what the Holy Spirit is accomplishing in the life of believers today.

SALVATION

- The Holy Spirit brings God's mercy to us (Hebrews 10:29).
- The Holy Spirit identifies us as God's own (Ephesians 1:13).
- We come to God through the Holy Spirit (Ephesians 2:18).
- The Holy Spirit lives in believers (Luke 2:25).
- The Holy Spirit is a foretaste of our future glory (Romans 8:32; 2 Corinthians 1:22; 2 Corinthians 5:5).
- It is the Holy Spirit that assigns our life work (Acts 20:28). The Holy Spirit enables us to experience the love of God (Romans 5:5; Romans 15:30; Colossians 1:8).
- As children of God, we overflow with confident hope through the power of the Holy Spirit (Romans 15:13).
- No one can say Jesus is Lord, except by the Holy Spirit.
- We prove ourselves (that we are children of God) by our purity, our understanding, our patience, our kindness by the Holy Spirit within us, and our sincere love (2 Corinthians 6:6, NLT).
- We know that God will give His Holy Spirit to those who ask Him (Luke 11:13).
- Aside from water baptism, there is a separate baptism of the Holy Spirit (Acts 1:5).

- The only sin that Jesus said would never be forgiven was blasphemy against the Holy Spirit (Matthew 12:31–32).

LIFE

- Through God's mercy, we have been given a new birth and a new life through the Holy Spirit (Titus 3:5).
- The Holy Spirit also gives birth to spiritual life (John 3:6). Our life in the Kingdom of God is described as a life of goodness and peace and joy in the Holy Spirit (Romans 14:17).
- The Holy Spirit is giving life (2 Corinthians 3:8).
- A believer's body is not his own; it has become the temple of the Holy Spirit (1 Corinthians 6:19).
- King David prayed that God's Holy Spirit would remain with Him (Psalm 51:11).
- Mary, the mother of Jesus, became pregnant by the power of the Holy Spirit (Matthew 1:18).

HOLINESS

- We are made holy by God's Holy Spirit (Romans 15:16).
- When we are dominated by the Spirit, we think about things that please the Spirit (Romans 8:5).
- By allowing the Holy Spirit to guide our lives, we won't do what our sinful nature craves (Galatians 5:16).
- The Holy Spirit produces love, joy, peace, patience, kindness, goodness, faithfulness, gentleness, and self-control.
- Instead of being drunk with wine, we can be filled with the Holy Spirit (Ephesians 5:18).

- It was through repentance and baptism in the Name of Jesus (for the forgiveness of sins) that many believers received God's Holy Spirit (Acts 2:38).

PRAYER

- We don't know what to pray for, but the Holy Spirit prays for us in an unknown language (Romans 8:26).
- The ability to speak in tongues is given by God's Holy Spirit (Acts 2:4).
- The Word of God admonishes us to pray in the power of the Holy Spirit (Jude 1:20).
- When believers received the Holy Spirit, they have spoken in other tongues and prophesied (Acts 19:6).
- Through worshipping the Lord and fasting, we are able to hear the Holy Spirit clearly (Acts 13:2).

TRUTH

- The Holy Spirit assures us of what is true (1 Thessalonians 1:5).
- The Holy Spirit teaches us everything and reminds us of what Jesus said (John 14:26).
- The Spirit teaches us everything we need to know, and what he teaches is true (1 John 2:27).
- It is the Holy Spirit who lives in us and leads us into all truth (John 14:17).
- The Holy Spirit prevents us from moving in the wrong direction (Acts 16:6).
- The Holy Spirit warns us and tells us of future events (Acts 20:23).

- It is because we believed the message we heard about Jesus Christ, that God has given us His Holy Spirit (Galatians 3:5).
- Jesus gave His apostles instructions through the Holy Spirit (Acts 1:2).

POWER AND BOLDNESS

- Jesus said the Holy Spirit would fill His disciples with power from heaven (Luke 24:49; Acts 1:8).
- The Holy Spirit speaks through us (Mark 13:11). Jesus Christ was filled with the Holy Spirit when He began His earthly ministry (Luke 4:1).
- It is the Holy Spirit who sends us out on God's assignments (Acts 13:4).
- The ability to communicate God's Word effectively is given by the Holy Spirit (1 Corinthians 6:19; 1 Peter 1:12–21).
- We come to God through the Holy Spirit (Ephesians 2:18).

MIRACLES

- God confirmed the message (about Christ) by giving signs and wonders and various miracles and gifts of the Holy Spirit whenever He chose (Hebrews 2:4).
- God anointed Jesus with the Holy Spirit and power, then Jesus went around doing good and healing all who were oppressed by the devil, for God was with Him (Acts 10:38).
- Jesus was raised from the dead by the power of the Holy Spirit (Romans 1:4).

- Saul was filled with the Holy Spirit and regained His sight when Ananias laid hands on him (Acts 9:17).
- When Peter and John laid their hands on believers, they too received the Holy Spirit (Acts 8:17).

PHYSICAL AND EMOTIONAL HEALING

It is God's will to heal. However, God has given us His Holy Spirit, through which He continues Christ's healing ministry in the earth realm. The Holy Spirit gives us the power to overcome anxiety, fear, and pain.

But if the Spirit of Him who raised Jesus from the dead dwells in you, He who raised Christ from the dead will also give life to your mortal bodies through His Spirit who dwells in you.

– Romans 8:11, NKJV

It is through our faith in Jesus and by acknowledging His Holy Spirit, that we receive our own emotional and physical healing.

As we love upon and trust in Jesus, we receive more of His Holy Spirit's power in our lives, hearts, bodies, and circumstances.

The Holy Spirit is overjoyed by our love for Christ, as He works to honor, support, and continue the ministry of Jesus Christ. Just as God has enormous reverence for the Holy Spirit, the Holy Spirit has great love and reverence for Christ Jesus.

In our determination to stand on the Word of God, we are relying on the power of the Holy Spirit. In fact, as we acknowledge the presence of the Holy Spirit within us, He manifests Himself by giving life to our mortal bodies.

LIVING BY HIS POWER

Our natural and spiritual lives are dependent upon the Holy Spirit. Unfortunately, man has not fully understood the importance of the Holy Spirit. However, we know that He raised Jesus from the dead and that He heals and strengthens our natural bodies. Therefore, life is in God's Spirit.

Additionally, it is the Holy Spirit who assigns our life work. Therefore, it should be our chief aim concerning our career, to discover the will of God.

Usually, God's will can be found in the areas where we have joy and peace because joy and peace are fruits of the Holy Spirit. All of us should be doing work that assists others and brings us joy.

Inevitably, we sometimes face roadblocks. The good news is that the mission God has given us cannot be stopped by outside forces. Through faith in Jesus, prayer, obedience, and prompt action, we can release the full power of God to achieve everything He has purposed for our loved ones and us.

Remember that it is our faith in Jesus and our reverence for God that intensifies the power of the Holy Spirit in our lives.

WHAT IT MEANS TO BE FILLED WITH THE SPIRIT

John the Baptist was filled with the Holy Spirit before his birth. Other powerful men and women of God were filled with the Holy Spirit as they heard the gospel, asked God for His spirit, or had hands laid upon them.

It is God's will that we are filled with His Holy Spirit because our bodies become His temple.

When we have faith in Jesus and earnestly desire the Spirit of God, He is given to us. God knows our hearts.

UNDERSTANDING THE MINISTRY OF THE HOLY SPIRIT

The modern church has put emphasis on God (in general) and salvation through Christ, but we have not understood how to maintain an intimate relationship with God the Trinity in all three (3) of His distinct persons.

The Bible makes it very clear how important the Holy Spirit is. Jesus Christ was empowered by the Spirit to withstand the devil, to teach, and do miracles. He told the apostles to wait for the Spirit before they launched their ministry.

Additionally, the Bible repeats that blasphemy against the Holy Spirit will never be forgiven. It is a serious matter to "grieve" the Holy Spirit by taking for granted Christ's great sacrifice for us.

> *And do not grieve the Holy Spirit of God, by whom*
> *you were sealed for the day of redemption.*
> – Ephesians 4:20, NKJV

Overall, the Bible portrays the Holy Spirit as loving, kind, and powerful, as He is fully God. He is responsible for bringing us to Christ and keeping us holy until Christ's return.

He assigns our lifework and gives us the power to accomplish all that God has put on our hearts to achieve. He heals our natural bodies and gives us eternal life through our faith in the love of Jesus Christ.

To Father God, we are His beloved children, the sons of God, and the daughters of God. It delights our Father God to give us His Holy Spirit who enables us to love with the love of God, speak the Word of God, know the future, and achieve all that God has called us to do.

The Bible tells us that the Holy Spirit is life itself. He is the Power of God in our lives; He is our Teacher, our Counselor, and our Helper. Therefore, we should cultivate a close fellowship with Him. We can talk to Him and, most importantly, listen to Him. It is through Him that we pray our most powerful prayers.

Grow closer to God's Holy Spirit, get to know Him, fall deeply in love with Him, and surrender your will to Him. He will enable you to succeed at every good work that God has put on your heart. He assists us in the salvation of others.

He has given us the ability to love others and He identifies us as children of God. His presence in our lives guarantees that we receive the honor God has for us on the day that Christ is revealed to the entire world.

2 WAYS WE CAN BECOME CLOSER TO GOD'S HOLY SPIRIT

1. **ASK** – Ask the Father, in the Name of Jesus, to fill you with the Holy Spirit.

2. **GIVE THANKS** – Just as we thank the Father and the Son through prayer, we should thank the Holy Spirit for living within us, strengthening us, and keeping us well.

When we are tempted with anxiety, fear, or pain, we should begin at once to thank and praise God for the power of the Holy Spirit that is within us.

The Spirit of God, who raised Jesus from the dead, lives in you. And just as God raised Christ Jesus from the dead, he will give life to your mortal bodies by this same Spirit living within you.

– Romans 8:11, NLT

UNDERSTAND PRAYING IN TONGUES

*O*ne great man of God said, "If I hadn't been filled with the Holy Spirit and began to pray in tongues, you never would have heard of me!" What he meant is that he received spiritual power that he didn't previously have.

> But you will receive power when the Holy Spirit comes
> upon you. And you will be my witnesses, telling people
> about me everywhere—in Jerusalem, throughout
> Judea, in Samaria, and to the ends of the earth.
>
> – Acts 1:8, NLT

To understand how vital the Holy Spirit is to our Christian life, remember that Jesus Christ Himself did not start His earthly ministry until He was filled with the Holy Spirit.

Additionally, he asked his disciples not to minister until they, too, were filled with the Holy Spirit. When Jesus left the earth, He left God's Holy Spirit to indwell us, counsel us, comfort us, and empower us.

PRAYING IN TONGUES

If you don't currently pray in tongues, if it is your desire, I believe that you can. Let's take a look at what the Word of God says concerning this matter.

Below are some of the frequently asked questions and vital scriptures on this important topic.

WHAT DOES THE BIBLE SAY ABOUT PRAYING IN TONGUES?

In Christ's day, Paul said everyone did not speak in tongues (1 Corinthians 12:30), although God gave His Church this gift.

> *And God has appointed these in the church:*
> *first apostles, second prophets, third teachers,*
> *after that miracles, then gifts of healings, helps,*
> *administrations, varieties of tongues.*
>
> – 1 Corinthians 12:28, NKJV

As we know, all these gifts can still be seen today (apostles, prophets, teachers, miracles, healings, helps, administrations, and tongues). For example, the gift of tongues was very prevalent in the days of the apostles, and it remains dominant today.

THERE CAN BE A SEPARATE INFILLING OF THE HOLY SPIRIT.

There is an infilling of the Holy Spirit where believers can begin to pray in tongues. This infilling may occur at the time of salvation or later through the laying on of hands.

*While Peter was still speaking these words, the
Holy Spirit fell upon all those who heard the word.
And those of the circumcision who believed were
astonished, as many as came with Peter, because the
gift of the Holy Spirit had been poured out on the
Gentiles also. For they heard them speak with tongues
and magnify God...*

– Acts 10:44-46, NKJV

*"Did you receive the Holy Spirit when you believed?"
he asked them. "No," they replied, "we haven't
even heard that there is a Holy Spirit." "Then what
baptism did you experience?" he asked. And they
replied, "The baptism of John." Paul said, "John's
baptism called for repentance from sin. But John
himself told the people to believe in the one who
would come later, meaning Jesus." As soon as they
heard this, they were baptized in the name of the
Lord Jesus. Then when Paul laid his hands on them,
the Holy Spirit came on them, and they spoke in other
tongues and prophesied. And when Paul had laid
hands on them, the Holy Spirit came upon them, and
they spoke with tongues and prophesied.*

– Acts 19:1-6, NKJV

WHY SHOULD I PRAY IN TONGUES?

There are many reasons that believers pray in tongues.
One reason is that it allows the Spirit of God to pray for
us. He prays for God's perfect will because we don't always

know what we should pray for. Another reason we should pray in tongues is that it strengthens us personally in spirit and in body.

> *Likewise, the Spirit also helps in our weaknesses. For we do not know what we should pray for as we ought, but the Spirit Himself makes intercession for us with groanings which cannot be uttered.*
>
> – Romans 8:26, NKJV

> *A person who speaks in tongues is strengthened personally, but one who speaks a word of prophecy strengthens the entire church.*
>
> – 1 Corinthians 14:4, NLT

In my personal life, I have found that God's Holy Spirit uses my prayers in tongues for these purposes: 1) to strengthen me physically and increase my confidence in God, 2) to release miracles in my life, 3) to overcome any adversity that is challenging me, 4) to give me wisdom and revelation knowledge while I pray, 5) to overcome obstacles, and 6) to pray for others.

The Word of God tells us that when the Holy Spirit was poured out on Christ's followers, they all received the ability to pray in unknown tongues. No one was left out.

This gift has not ceased. Even today, thousands (perhaps millions) of Christians across the globe pray in unknown tongues during corporate prayer (in church) or in private.

Why should anyone pray in tongues? We pray in tongues because the Bible tells us that it allows the Holy Spirit to fluently pray through us (Romans 8:26).

Allowing the Holy Spirit to pray through us will enable us to receive deliverance and healing and remove road-blocks to our success.

The Apostle Paul said he prayed both ways. He prayed in the language that was understood, and he prayed in tongues (in the Spirit). In fact, he prayed in tongues more than any of his contemporaries. Paul is considered one of the most powerful apostles who ever lived!

> *Well then, what shall I do? I will pray in the spirit, and I will also pray in words I understand. I will sing in the spirit, and I will also sing in words I understand.*
>
> – 1 Corinthians 14:15, NLT

> *I thank God that I speak in tongues more than any of you.*
>
> – 1 Corinthians 14:18, NLT

God's Word tells us to desire the good gifts of the Spirit and to be careful not to stifle the Holy Spirit.

> *Do not quench [subdue, or be unresponsive to the working and guidance of] the [Holy] Spirit.*
>
> – 1 Thessalonians 5:19, AMP

Every believer should flow with the Spirit of God and be open to receive all that will empower God in their life. I sincerely believe that each of us can have a much more powerful and more purposeful life in Christ through the gift of praying in tongues.

Additionally, I don't believe that the gift is denied to anyone. Many believers ask God for the gift of praying in tongues and many (like myself) have received it.

I received the ability to pray in tongues when hands were laid on me, but I longed for the gifts of the Spirit, welcomed them, and prayed to receive and keep them.

I felt confident that the gifts of the Spirit would enable me to live a more faith-filled, effective, and intimate life in Christ. However, I had to deliberately have faith that God could pray in tongues through me.

If I had not earnestly desired the infilling of the Holy Spirit, I would have stifled or stopped the flow of God's Spirit in this area of my life.

Now, I regularly pray in tongues to release the power of God over my life and the lives of others. Over time, the Spirit of God has confirmed to me during many instances that He is truly praying through me.

I would encourage any new or seasoned Christian to receive the baptism of the Holy Spirit with the power to speak in tongues. I truly believe that it will add immeasurable dimensions of power to your relationship with God and your Christian life.

FROM A BIBLICAL PERSPECTIVE, CAN ANY BELIEVER BEGIN TO PRAY IN TONGUES?

I believe the answer to that question is yes! But, first, the Bible tells us to earnestly desire the good gifts of the Spirit.

> But earnestly desire the best gifts. And yet I show you a more excellent way.
>
> – 1 Corinthians 12:31, NKJV

The second reason we can be confident that God will allow any believer to pray in tongues is that He promised to give His Spirit to anyone who asks.

If you then, being evil, know how to give good gifts to your children, how much more will your heavenly Father give the Holy Spirit to those who ask Him!

– Luke 11:13, NKJV

Thousands of believers never speak in the Holy Spirit because they have never asked God for this good gift!

The Word of God says that God has no favorites, and He never shows favoritism (1 Peter 1:17). This is true because many thousands have purposefully asked God for the ability to pray in tongues, and it has been granted to them!

HOW CAN I BEGIN TO PRAY IN TONGUES?

First, repent of all sins, for God said He gives His Spirit to those who obey Him (Acts 5:32). Second, God promised to give His Spirit to anyone who asks (Luke 11:13).

Therefore, we can ask Him for the infilling of the Holy Spirit with the ability to pray in tongues. Finally, speaking in tongues can be given through the laying on of hands. Therefore, any Spirit-filled believer (who prays in tongues) can lay their hands on you, and you can expect to pray in tongues with them!

Do not struggle to pray in tongues. All that is required is that you earnestly desire this good gift and believe (have faith) that you have received it.

It is helpful to pray in the Holy Spirit with another Spirit-filled believer. Remember, the Holy Spirit will not force your mouth open; you will have to start speaking, and He will give you His words!

Today, many believers have received the ability to pray in unknown tongues as the Holy Spirit gives them utterance. However, the Holy Spirit does not insist that any believer prays in tongues, but this special infilling of the Spirit is not withheld from those who earnestly desire it.

THE HOLY SPIRIT CONFIRMS PRAYING IN TONGUES

Finally, I will share a personal testimony.

Shortly after giving my life to Christ, I was at home kneeling and praying in tongues for the first few times in my life. I was a bit nervous and not sure I was praying as God intended.

However, a minister at my church said this to me, "Keep praying in tongues, and don't let the devil tell you that you aren't praying in tongues!"

How did he know? That is precisely what the enemy was doing. Each time I would pray in tongues, he placed doubt in my mind to stop me.

Taking the minister's advice, I kept praying in tongues with great authority and faith. While I was praying, the telephone on my nightstand rang. I shouldn't have answered it, but for some reason, I picked up the phone.

It was a man who worked at the building where I resided. He was calling me to let me know I had a package downstairs.

However, when I said hello, he said, "When you picked up the phone and started talking, I felt like a bolt of lightning went through me!" All I could say in response was, "Really?" Then he proceeded to tell me about the package. We were both stunned.

When I got off the phone, I was amazed and wondered what the Holy Spirit was trying to tell me. In my heart, God's reply was, "I wanted you to have proof that you are really praying in the Holy Spirit – with power!"

From that day forward, I never again stopped praying in tongues, nor have I doubted that the Holy Spirit is changing circumstances for good through my prayers.

I know that through our faith, the Holy Spirit can utilize our tongues to pray the will of God into the earth realm.

If you do not desire to pray in tongues, rest assured that you can still live a wonderful Christian life and go to heaven. For the greatest gift and the best gift we have all been given is love.

A MORE PERFECT GIFT

The Word of God says that one day our human knowledge and some gifts will fade away – except for love!

Love never fails. But where there are prophecies, they will cease; where there are tongues, they will be restrained; where there is knowledge, it will be dismissed.

– 1 Corinthians 13:8, BSB

Three things will last forever—faith, hope, and love— and the greatest of these is love.

– 1 Corinthians 13:13, NLT

END PAIN FROM ABANDONMENT & ABUSE

THE SEVEN STEPS TO FREEDOM

*W*e can overcome the deep emotional pain and depression caused by living with abandonment, neglect, and abuse. Here's what our Lord said.

> *"For I know the plans I have for you," declares the LORD, "plans to prosper you and not to harm you, plans to give you hope and a future."*
>
> - Jeremiah 29:11, NIV

Our earthly father may have been imperfect, but God said He's our real father!

> *A father of the fatherless, a defender of widows, is God in His holy habitation.*
>
> – Psalm 68:5, NKJV

Furthermore, if we are saved, we have a new family – the family of God. As Christians, we must accept that we put our biological roots behind us. We love our families of origin, but they no longer bind us.

> *This means that anyone who belongs to Christ has become a new person. The old life is gone; a new life has begun!*
>
> – 2 Corinthians 5:17, NLT

In my own life, at one time, I felt very sorrowful when I considered the heartbreak of the past. At times, I would cry, and at other times, I felt angry toward those who unjustly hurt me.

> *But when you are praying, first forgive anyone you are holding a grudge against, so that your Father in heaven will forgive your sins, too.*
>
> – Mark 11:25, NLT

It wasn't until I began to study the Bible in earnest that I was entirely healed by Christ. I still remember the past, but it no longer hurts. I am focused on the future and no longer bound by my past.

Honestly, all that is required to heal past wounds is to be taught the Word of God.

Then, if your mind is renewed with the Word of God, you would be set free. But, unfortunately, it requires faith to study the Word of God and receive transformation.

> *Nothing is impossible for God!*
>
> – -Luke 1:37, CEV

If you can believe, all things are possible to him who believes.

– Mark 9:23, NKJV

We can be healed of any physical or emotional sickness; we can take our life back and look forward to a glorious future.

You didn't choose me. I chose you. I appointed you to go and produce lasting fruit so that the Father will give you whatever you ask for, using my name.

– John 15:16, NLT

Again, all that is required is a mustard seed of faith.

Every day, people commit suicide because they do not know how to escape the present challenges, forget the past, or believe in God for a brighter future.

Joy can be restored! Health can be restored!

I shall not die, but live, And declare the works of the LORD.

– Psalm 118:17, NKJV

All God has asked the grieving person to do is to saturate their mind in the Word of God. Study the Bible and be set free. You will know the truth, and the truth will set you free (John 8:32).

Here are seven (7) tips that set us free of the past if we will dare to believe in Christ and act on them.

1. **WE MUST REPENT**: We must repent of anger, rage, bitterness, and our lack of faith in God's ability to do everything we can't do.

89

2. **WE MUST HUMBLE OURSELVES:** We must not harden our hearts so that we cannot receive the love of Christ, which heals our spirit, body, and soul. Many people have hardened their hearts toward anything that would offer hope. It's this unbelief and unyielding hardness (against the good promises of God) that keep us bound in misery.

3. **WE MUST FORGIVE OURSELVES:** We must forgive ourselves for the part we played in the past mistakes. If we don't forgive ourselves for bitterness, rage, unforgiveness, and mistakes, we can't forgive others.

4. **WE MUST FORGIVE OUR ABUSERS:** This is a command of God. It is non-negotiable. Often, we have been abused by more than one person. It is helpful to come before God in prayer and list their names in writing. Then, one by one, forgive them and ask God to forgive them, too. Pray that they will one day be saved and come to know God.

But if you refuse to forgive others, your Father will not forgive your sins.
– Matthew 6:15, NLT

But I say, love your enemies! Pray for those who persecute you!
– Matthew 5:44, NLT

But to you who are willing to listen, I say, love your enemies! Do good to those who hate you.
– Luke 6:27, NLT

5. **WE MUST CREATE BOUNDARIES:** God does not ask us to live with or be friends with abusers. It is best to

create distance from people who hurt us and bring out the worst in us. We don't have to stop speaking. We can be kind over the telephone. But we have no obligation to allow anyone to further disrespect and abuse us. We should not continue to be angry with anyone, instead, we should continue to pray for their salvation.

6. **WE MUST CONFESS (OUT LOUD) WHO WE ARE IN CHRIST:** Who we are in Christ is our new identity. Knowing what we have inherited as children of God will transform our entire life. (See the chapter Who We Are In Christ and read this list daily for a month. You will become a new person!)

7. **WE MUST RENEW OUR MINDS WITH THE WORD OF GOD:** God tells us to study the Word so that we will know His perfect will for our lives.

Don't copy the behavior and customs of this world, but let God transform you into a new person by changing the way you think. Then you will learn to know God's will for you, which is good and pleasing and perfect.

– Romans 12:2, NLT

In summary, I promise you that you can be healed in spirit, body, and soul.

You can be relieved of ill health, pain, anxiety, and depression. God earnestly wants to restore your life, restore your health, and restore your joy if only you dare to believe it!

"What do you mean, 'If I can'?" Jesus asked.
"Anything is possible if a person believes."

Mark 9:23, NLT

DIVINE HEALING
IN A NUTSHELL

The Word of God tells us that God has already given us everything we need.

Additionally, He promised us that He has already given us the victory. This victory is received through our faith.

> I have told you these things, so that in Me you may have [perfect] peace and confidence. In the world you have tribulation and trials and distress and frustration; but be of good cheer [take courage; be confident, certain, undaunted]! For I have overcome the world. [I have deprived it of power to harm you and have conquered it for you.]
>
> – John 16:33, AMPC

> By his divine power, God has given us everything we need to live a godly life. We have received all

of this by coming to know him, the one who called us to himself by means of his marvelous glory and excellence.

– 2 Peter 1:3, NLT

For every child of God defeats this evil world, and we achieve this victory through our faith.

– 1 John 5:4, NLT

God did not promise that we would not be challenged. In fact, Jesus himself was tempted and tested while on earth. Jesus was tempted in the same areas as us. However, He believed God and obeyed God.

This High Priest of ours understands our weaknesses, for he faced all of the same testings we do, yet he did not sin.

– Hebrews 4:15, NLT

If God has given us everything we need for victory in life, why are we suffering? The Lord said it is because "We lack knowledge and we don't know Him" (Hosea 4:6).

The Word of God tells us that we can call for the elders of the church, and they can pray for us. In this way, we may receive immediately healing.

However, suppose we never learn to pray for ourselves and others. In that case, we may have no defense if that illness or something else challenges us in the future. It is wonderful to receive prayer and excellent to pray with a firm believer in prayer. Nonetheless, we should learn to pray independently and for others.

TEN KEYS TO DIVINE HEALING

1. **SALVATION** - Most importantly, we confess Jesus as the Son of God, our Savior, and the Lord of our lives. When we become children of God, His Holy Spirit, His covenant promises, and His blessing are ours. Saving our souls is more important than healing our bodies. We must set our hearts to walk in love with others and in obedience to God. When we fall out of fellowship with God, we often lose our confidence to have faith in Him for miracles. However, God understands and accepts our repentance when we fall short. His love is unconditional, and He wants us well!

2. **KNOWLEDGE** – We should study the Word of God on divine healing until we understand its principles. We learn how to apply the Word of God to our situation. Practice makes perfect, and this is the skill we use for our entire life to remain well and help others recover.

3. **THE WORD OF GOD** – We should meditate on the Word of God (Biblical scriptures) until it gets in our hearts and we fully understand its power over our circumstances. The more we focus on Jesus alone and meditate on His words, the more power we wield over the enemy and every threat of sickness.

4. **FAITH** – We must believe that the Word of God will release miracles in our lives. Everything we study, practice, and act upon requires faith in God and His Word to be effective. As we know, God and His Word

95

are one. In divine healing, we are standing firmly on the truth of His Biblical Word.

5. **THE NAME OF JESUS** – Jesus commanded us to use His Name to release His power, just as the apostles did. There are excellent books that explain the power in the Name of Jesus. One of the most influential books is *The Wonderful Name of Jesus* by E. W. Kenyon.

6. **CONFESSION** – We must speak the Word of God over our symptoms, body, and thought life. We must never contradict God's Word or have two confessions. We must acknowledge that we are healed to ourselves and to others, even in the face of contradictory evidence.

7. **SPIRITUAL AUTHORITY** – We should use the power and authority that Jesus gave us to orally cast out demons of fear, infirmity, and pain. This is not difficult. Demons are under our feet, and they fear the Word of God. All we need to say is, "In the Name of Jesus, I command you to leave my body!" When we believe in the power of the Name of Jesus and the Word of God, we know demons must leave.

8. **PERSISTENCE** – Regardless of our symptoms or diagnosis, we continue to believe God and recite His word until we have complete victory. We must always exalt the Word of God over our circumstances, no matter how dire they may seem.

9. **PRAISE AND THANKSGIVING** – Throughout our recovery and for the rest of our lives, we praise and thank God daily. We thank Him for saving us,

healing us, and setting us free from the bondage of fear and sickness.

10. **ACTION** – Our faith is demonstrated and proved when we act on the Word of God. If we hear the Word and do nothing to act on it, it becomes useless.

SUMMARY

Christians who have sought God for divine healing have been spared death, operations, and life-long addiction to drug therapy. And, in the process, God does away with the financial loss and anguish, too.

Having faith in God and trusting in Him for our healing isn't nearly as hard as visiting doctors, receiving a troubling diagnosis, paying for treatments and drugs, and undergoing procedures.

> **Learning and acting upon God's promises is far easier than anything else we could do to be healed.**

The good news is that when we begin to follow God, He blesses us, and we start to feel the improvement almost immediately. Some people are healed instantly!

HINDRANCES TO HEALING

10 ROADBLOCKS TO AVOID

*D*ivine healing of the physical body and emotions is not tricky. However, even God requires that we participate in our own wellness. At times, we must focus on achieving a worthwhile goal.

It's not our fault that we got sick or are sick. God knows we live in a fallen world.

That is why He gave us Jesus, the Holy Spirit, and the Word of God to heal us!

Below are a few of the traps that keep believers in a sick condition.

The good news is that we can avoid every one of them! It's not complicated. All Jesus ever asked for was a mustard seed of faith.

"You don't have enough faith," Jesus told them. *"I tell you the truth, if you had faith even as small as a mustard seed, you could say to this mountain, 'Move from here to there,' and it would move. Nothing would be impossible."*

– Matthew 17:20, NLT

Take a look at this list and candidly ask yourself if you have any of these defeating conditions.

Remember, God is on our side. If we decide to trust in Him, He will give us all we need to succeed. All He needs is a humble, yielded heart.

So do not fear, for I am with you; do not be dismayed, for I am your God. I will strengthen you and help you; I will uphold you with my righteous right hand.

– Isaiah 41:10, NIV

Is any of this holding you back?

1. **A LACK OF KNOWLEDGE**: Not knowing the Word of God concerning divine healing. Not knowing healing scriptures. Not meditating on the Word of God.

2. **TAKING NO ACTION**: Knowing the Word but not acting on it. Giving mental assent without doing anything.

3. **UNBELIEF**: Knowing God is divinely healing others but refusing to believe He will heal you. Refusing to

receive or develop a personal relationship with God's Holy Spirit.

4. **UNFORGIVENESS:** Anger, resentment, unforgiveness, and bitterness against others. Grief over our losses and the past. A wish to die.

5. **GUILT:** Deliberately continuing to sin without repentance.

6. **WRONG CONFESSION:** Having two opposing confessions – confessing to friends, family, and doctors that we are sick, then saying we believe we are healed by Jesus' stripes. Repeating that we are ill or have a disease or condition. Agreeing with evil medical reports and failing to speak the Word of God instead.

7. **DECEPTION:** Allowing physical symptoms to convince us that the Word of God is not working for us.

8. **IDOLATRY:** Completely relying on the wisdom of man (science) instead of using our faith in Jesus for natural healing. Pride and failure to humble ourselves before God.

9. **BONDAGE:** Asking God for a miracle, but being unwilling to stop abusing our body with food, drugs, alcohol, or other addictive substances. A refusal to keep fasting until every addiction and source of bondage is broken (food, alcohol, drug addiction). Not knowing how to cast out an evil spirit.

10. **PITY:** Holding onto sickness for attention, companionship, pity, stipends, or to inspire guilt in significant others.

In my own life, I've found that avoiding these potential roadblocks to healing isn't really hard. All of us make mistakes.

The benefits of doing things God's way are enormous. However, we must realize that excellent health, joy, and being free of pain are priceless!

WHO WE ARE IN CHRIST

But as it is written, Eye hath not seen, nor ear heard, neither have entered into the heart of man, the things which God hath prepared for them that love him.

– 1 Corinthians 2:9, KJB

When I got saved, I had no idea that everything I wanted to become through Christianity I already possessed – in Christ. Below are a few of the promises of God that will elevate the faith, effectiveness, and success of every believer.

If you meditate on these truths daily, they will transform your entire life!

For thirty days, confess out loud who you are in Christ. Then, when the promises of God become embedded in your heart, they will transform your life and renew your thinking. The Word of God is powerful and alive!

Read and meditate on what the Word of God has said about us.

———

WHO I AM IN CHRIST

- I am born again (1 Peter 1:23)
- I am a child of God (1 John 3:1-2)
- I have been set free (John 8:32-36)
- As Christ is, so am I in this world (1 John 4:17)
- I am greatly loved by God (Romans 8:38-39)
- I am precious and honored (Isaiah 43:4)
- I have the power to produce wealth and be successful (Deuteronomy 8:18)
- I am a son of God (or daughter) (Galatians 3:26-27)
- I am the temple of God, and the Spirit of God lives in me (1 Corinthians 6:19)
- Christ, Himself lives in me (Galatians 2:20)
- I am a minister of reconciliation between God and people (2 Corinthians 5:18)
- God has given me gifts and a call (Romans 11:29)
- I am sanctified and called to holiness (1 Corinthians 1-2)
- I am a new creature, a whole new creation in Christ (2 Corinthians 5:17)
- I belong to a chosen people, a royal priesthood, and a holy nation (1 Peter 2:9)
- I am justified, redeemed, and forgiven (Romans 3:23-24)
- I am the righteousness of God in Christ (2 Corinthians 5:21)

- I am righteous and holy (Ephesians 4:24)
- I am never alone because God will never leave me (Hebrews 13:5)
- I am freed from all bondage by the Spirit of the Lord (2 Corinthians 3:17)
- I am blessed (Ephesians 1:3)
- I am one with the Lord (1 Corinthians 6:17)
- I am more than a conqueror (Romans 8:37)
- I have become a child of God (John 1:12)
- I am God's possession (1 Corinthians 6:20)
- I am one of God's saints (Ephesians 1:1)
- I am Christ's friend (John 15:15)
- I am God's ambassador (2 Corinthians 5:20)
- God chose me (Ephesians 1:4-6)
- I am God's beloved (2 Thessalonians 2:13)
- I am complete in Him (Colossians 2:10)
- I am victorious through Jesus Christ (1 Corinthians 15:57)
- I am being kept, guarded, and protected (1 Peter 1:5)
- I am seated in heavenly places (Ephesians 2:6)
- I am the head and not the tail (Deuteronomy 28:13)
- I am the salt of the earth and the light of the world (Matthew 5:13-14)
- I am healed by His stripes (Isaiah 53:5)

MY POWER - WHAT I CAN DO

- I can do all things through Christ who strengthens me (Philippians 4:13)
- I have authority over all the power of the enemy, and nothing can harm me (Luke 10:19)

- I can come boldly and confidently into God's presence because of my faith in Christ (Ephesians 3:12)
- I can chase a thousand, for the Lord my God fights for me (Joshua 23:10)
- I turn all my cares, anxieties, and worries over to Christ because He cares about me with the deepest affection and watches over me very carefully (1 Peter 5:7 AMP)
- I can come boldly to the throne of God to receive mercy and find grace (Hebrews 4:16)
- I always triumph in Christ Jesus (2 Corinthians 2:14)

POSSESSIONS – WHAT I ALREADY RECEIVED FROM CHRIST

- There is no condemnation against me, and I've been set free (Romans 8:1-2)
- My God shall fully supply all my needs (Philippians 4:19)
- I have faith (Romans 12:3)
- I have eternal life (John 10:27-28)
- Our God gives us riches and wealth (Ecclesiastes 5:19)
- No one can stand against me or be victorious against me (Romans 8:31)
- I have the joy of the Lord as my strength (Nehemiah 8:10)
- I have peace because my mind is focused on the Lord (Isaiah 26:3)
- I have the mind of Christ (1 Corinthians 2:16)
- God gave me His Spirit of power, love, and self-control (2 Timothy 1:7)

- My sleep is sweet (Proverbs 3:24)
- I have peace with God Himself (Romans 5:1)
- I have direct access to the Father God (Romans 5:2)
- God keeps me safe, and the evil one cannot harm or touch me (1 John 5:18)
- I have been given wisdom and understanding (Ephesians 1:8)
- I have everything I need for life and godliness (2 Peter 1:3)
- I am chosen, holy, set apart, blameless (Ephesians 1:4)
- I am forgiven (Colossians 2:13)
- I have been given the Holy Spirit (2 Corinthians 1:22)
- I have been given God's great and precious promises (2 Peter 1:4)
- The Lord will rescue me from every trap (Psalm 91:3)
- No plague can come near my dwelling (Psalm 91:10)
- Angles protect me wherever I go (Psalm 91:11)
- When I call on the Lord, He will answer because I love Him (Psalm 91:15)

———

WHAT CANNOT HAPPEN

- I cannot be separated from God's unlimited love (Romans 8:39)
- When I am born of God, I do not sin because I have become righteous in Christ (1 John 5:18)

God saved you by his grace when you believed. And you can't take credit for this; it is a gift from God.
— Ephesians 2:8, NLT

POWERFUL HEALING SCRIPTURES

THE PROMISES OF GOD

For the Word of God is living and powerful, and sharper than any two-edged sword, piercing even to the division of soul and spirit, and of joints and marrow, and is a discerner of the thoughts and intents of the heart.

– Hebrews 4:12, NKJV

*T*o crush anxiety, fear, and pain, it is necessary to know the Word of God concerning divine healing. In fact, there are essential core scriptures that should be memorized, meditated on, and repeated during the day.

It is the Word of God that removes anxiety and all manner of sickness.

TO OVERCOME ANXIETY, FEAR, AND PAIN, HERE ARE FOUR TIPS FOR VICTORY.

1. We must know the Word of God on divine healing.

2. We must meditate on these words until they become a part of us.

3. We must believe the Word of God.

4. We must speak the Word of God in the form of healing scriptures over our bodies several times a day.

One powerful companion to reciting healing scriptures over our bodies is taking Holy Communion at home each day and thanking God for our healing.

MEDITATE ON AND MEMORIZE THESE CORE SCRIPTURES ABOUT HEALING.

Surely He took on our infirmities and carried our sorrows; yet we considered Him stricken by God, struck down and afflicted. But He was pierced for our transgressions, He was crushed for our iniquities; the punishment that brought us peace was upon Him, and by His stripes we are healed.

– Isaiah 53:4-5, BSB

He Himself bore our sins in His body on the tree, so that we might die to sin and live to righteousness. "By His stripes you are healed."

– 1 Peter 2:24, BSB

That evening many demon-possessed people were brought to Jesus. He cast out the evil spirits with a simple command, and he healed all the sick. This fulfilled the word of the Lord through the prophet Isaiah, who said, "He took our sicknesses and removed our diseases."

– Matthew 8:16-17, NLT

Look, I have given you authority over all the power of the enemy, and you can walk among snakes and scorpions and crush them. Nothing will injure you.

– Luke 10:19, NLT

This means that anyone who belongs to Christ has become a new person. The old life is gone; a new life has begun!

– 2 Corinthians 5:17, NLT

I shall not die, but live, And declare the works of the LORD.

– Psalm 118:17, NKJV

If we confess our sins, he is faithful and just to forgive us our sins, and to cleanse us from all unrighteousness.

– 1 John 1:9, KJB

For God has not given us a spirit of fear and timidity, but of power, love, and self-discipline.

– 2 Timothy 1:7, NLT

For with God nothing will be impossible."

— Luke 1:37, NKJV

The Spirit of God, who raised Jesus from the dead, lives in you. And just as God raised Christ Jesus from the dead, he will give life to your mortal bodies by this same Spirit living within you.

— Romans 8:11, NLT

Then Christ will make his home in your hearts as you trust in him. Your roots will grow down into God's love and keep you strong.

— Ephesians 3:17, NLT

He sent out his word and healed them, snatching them from the door of death.

— Psalm 107:20, NLT

I shall not die, but live, And declare the works of the LORD.

— Psalm 118:17, NKJV

You will keep in perfect peace all who trust in you, all whose thoughts are fixed on you!

— Isaiah 26:3, NLT

Give all your worries and cares to God, for he cares about you.

— 1 Peter 5:7, NLT

By this is love perfected with us, so that we may have confidence for the day of judgment, because as he is so also are we in this world.

– 1 John 4:17, ESV

ADDITIONAL HEALING SCRIPTURES FOR ADDED POWER:

Is anyone among you sick? Let them call the elders of the church to pray over them and anoint them with oil in the name of the Lord. And the prayer offered in faith will make the sick person well; the Lord will raise them up. If they have sinned, they will be forgiven.

– James 5:14-15, NIV

For God has not given us a spirit of cowardice, but of power, and of love, and of self-control.

– 2 Timothy 1:7, BLB

You shall serve the LORD your God, and he will bless your bread and your water, and I will take sickness away from among you. None shall miscarry or be barren in your land; I will fulfill the number of your days.

– Exodus 23:25-26, ESV

All praise to God, the Father of our Lord Jesus Christ, who has blessed us with every spiritual blessing in the heavenly realms because we are united with Christ.

– Ephesians 1:3, NLT

*But You are holy, O You who are enthroned in [the
holy place where] the praises of Israel [are offered].*

– Psalm 22:3, AMP

*And my God shall supply all your need according to
His riches in glory by Christ Jesus.*

– Philippians 4:19, NKJV

Jesus Christ is the same yesterday, today, and forever.

– Hebrews 13:8, NLT

*I tell you the truth, whatever you forbid on earth will
be forbidden in heaven, and whatever you permit on
earth will be permitted in heaven.*

– Matthew 18:18, NLT

*Verily I say unto you, Whatsoever ye shall bind on
earth shall be bound in heaven: and whatsoever ye
shall loose on earth shall be loosed in heaven.*

– Matthew 18:18, KJB

*If you openly declare that Jesus is Lord and believe
in your heart that God raised him from the dead, you
will be saved.*

– Romans 10:9, NLT

*But you belong to God, my dear children. You have
already won a victory over those people, because the
Spirit who lives in you is greater than the spirit who
lives in the world.*

– 1 John 4:4, NLT

Don't love money; be satisfied with what you have.
For God has said, "I will never fail you. I will never
abandon you."

– Hebrews 13:5, NLT

But don't rejoice because evil spirits obey you; rejoice
because your names are registered in heaven.

– Luke 10:20, NLT

For he raised us from the dead along with Christ and
seated us with him in the heavenly realms because we
are united with Christ Jesus.

– Ephesians 2:6, NLT

I have told you these things, so that in Me you
may have [perfect] peace. In the world you have
tribulation and distress and suffering, but be
courageous [be confident, be undaunted, be filled
with joy]; I have overcome the world." [My conquest
is accomplished, My victory abiding.]

– John 16:33, AMP

We know how much God loves us, and we have put
our trust in his love. God is love, and all who live in
love live in God, and God lives in them.

– 1 John 4:16, NLT

News about him spread as far as Syria, and people soon
began bringing to him all who were sick. And whatever
their sickness or disease, or if they were demon
possessed or epileptic or paralyzed—he healed them all.

– Matthew 4:24, NLT

God made him who had no sin to be sin for us, so that in him we might become the righteousness of God.

– 2 Corinthians 5:21, NIV

I love you, LORD; you are my strength.

– Psalm 18:1, NLT

O LORD, if you heal me, I will be truly healed; if you save me, I will be truly saved. My praises are for you alone!

– Jeremiah 17:14, NLT

Christ redeemed us from the curse of the law by becoming a curse for us, for it is written: "Cursed is everyone who is hung on a pole."

– Galatians 3:13, NIV

———

Meditating God's healing promises, believing them, and speaking them over our bodies can eradicate sickness and infuse us with life.

This works because the word of life is alive. God and His word are one, and God's word cannot fail.

For the Word of God is living and powerful, and sharper than any two-edged sword, piercing even to the division of soul and spirit, and of joints and marrow, and is a discerner of the thoughts and intents of the heart.

– Hebrews 4:12, NKJV

In the beginning was the Word, and the Word was with God, and the Word was God.

— John 1:1, NKJV

So shall My word be that goes forth from My mouth; It shall not return to Me void, But it shall accomplish what I please, And it shall prosper in the thing for which I sent it.

— Isaiah 55:11, NKJV

Faith and patience are twins. If we meditate on the word, believe it, and speak it, we will see miracles of healing in our lives and in the lives of our loved ones!

DAILY CONFESSION FOR HEALING

It is by confessing the Word of God over our situation and without backing down that we are healed. Our healing may appear instantly or progressively over time.

A powerful tool that is often utilized by believers is a daily confession of God's Word. Here are three benefits of reciting our daily confession.

1. Our daily confession is a shield against satanic attacks.

2. Our daily confession uplifts our spirits and releases great faith in the Word of God. The Lord said, "You will have what you say."

3. Our daily confession actually speaks to the cells, atoms, and tissues of our bodies and directs them to be healed.

DAILY CONFESSION TO WALK IN DIVINE HEALTH

God's Word is my medicine! It will bring heath and healing to all my flesh and bones. I will never cower before sickness, for God did not give me a spirit of fear. Instead, He gave me a Spirit of power, love, and a sound mind.

Therefore, in the Name of Jesus, I submit to God's Word, and I resist every spirit of fear because nothing can harm me, hurt me, or cause me pain.

Christ has given me authority and power to cast out demons and, over all, the power of the devil. Therefore, in the mighty Name of Jesus, I command the spirits of fear, unbelief, torment, and death to shut up and flee – now!!!

God's Word said He will forbid [or bind] what I forbid, and He will allow [or let loose] anything I allow. Therefore, I forbid any trace of sickness, disease, or pain to manifest or remain in my body. In the Name of Jesus, pain, illness, sickness, disease, and demons – leave my body NOW!

In 1 Peter 2:24, the Spirit of God said, "By Jesus' wounds, I was healed."

That confirms that I am healed right now! Let God be true, and every opposing person be a liar. I decree and declare that I AM NOT SICK ANYMORE in the Name of Jesus because God's Word is true, and the truth has set me free! My body is marvelous and wonderfully made. Right now, I have a robust miraculous body. I can do all things through Christ who strengthens me! I bind and forbid every thought, feeling, report, or confession of sickness to linger in my thought life or body.

In Mark 11:23, Jesus said I can have whatever I say and honestly believe. I genuinely believe in the Word of God.

Every Word of God profits me because I mix His Word with faith. Therefore, in the mighty Name of Jesus, I decree that:

- God is the LORD that heals me. I exalt His Word over all the wisdom of man.
- The Word of God is my medicine, and it always works because God is not a liar. He watches over His Word and hastens to perform it!
- Nothing is impossible for God or for me because I believe.
- I am not too sick, too far gone, or too old to walk in divine health because the Spirit of God in me is stronger [and more powerful] than anything [or any devil] in the world.
- I know that God is able to accomplish more than I can ask or think!
- I have confidence in God's love for me because I confess my sins to God, and He is faithful and just to forgive me.
- I walk in love with others to fulfill God's whole law, knowing that faith works by love. I will enjoy life and see good days because I repent of saying cruel things or telling lies.
- I am righteous and in right standing with God, through my faith in the finished work of Christ. All my sins are covered in the blood of Jesus.
- I am redeemed from the curses of sickness, disease, pain, and premature death.

- By Jesus' wounds, I was already healed and made whole. I am perfectly well right now. I will talk like it and act like it!
- My food is blessed, consecrated, sanctified, and purified by the Word of God and prayer. Nothing I eat or drink will make me sick.
- God has taken sickness away from me.
- Nothing will hurt me, harm me, injure me, or cause me pain.
- I fear no evil, for God is with me.
- I love and trust Jesus, and He has blessed me with a long good life.

All praise to God, who has [already] blessed me with every spiritual blessing in the heavenly realms because I am united with Christ!

Scriptures Confessed Above: Exodus 15:26, Proverbs 4:20-22, 2 Timothy 1:17, Luke 10:19, Matthew 18:18, 1 Peter 2:24, Romans 3:4, John 8:31-32, Philippians 4:13, Mark 11:23, Hebrews 4:2, Psalms 103:70, Numbers 23:19, Jeremiah 1:12, Luke 1:37, Mark 9:23, Matthew 17:20, 1 John 4:4, Ephesians 3:20, 1 John 1:9, Romans 10:13, Galatians 5:6, 1 Peter 3:10, 2 Corinthians 5:21, Galatians 3:13, Isaiah 53:5, 1 Timothy 4:4-5, Exodus 23:25, Psalms 23:4, Psalms 91:16, Psalms 23:6, Ephesians 3:20.

BE SAVED AND HEALED!

A PRAYER OF FAITH

Therefore, confess your sins to one another [your false steps, your offenses], and pray for one another, that you may be healed and restored. The heartfelt and persistent prayer of a righteous man (believer) is able to accomplish much [when put into action and made effective by God—it is dynamic and can have tremendous power].

– James 5:16, AMP

Speak Healing.

WHAT WE SAY WHEN WE ARE ALONE IS HEARD BY AN AUDIENCE.

1. God hears our thoughts and our words.

2. Our holy guardian angels hear our spoken words and react to them.

3. Our bodies hear what we say and believe. Organs react to those words.

4. Even unclean spirits hear our words and react to them.

Read the below prayer. To receive healing, say it out loud and with faith and conviction. Remember that God, angels, and even evil spirits hear us, and they respond.

PRAYER TO RECEIVE HEALING:

"Father God, in the Name of Jesus, I thank you for your unfailing love, mercy, and faithfulness. I believe that Jesus Christ is your Son and He died on the cross to pay for my sins. Therefore, Father, I repent of every sin and I forgive those who have sinned against me.

Lord, Jesus, come into my heart. Live your life in me and through me from this day forward. Fill me with your precious Holy Spirit and the ability to love as you love and believe as you believe.

Lord, you said that whatever I ask for in the Name of Jesus would be done for me. Therefore, in the Name of Jesus, Father accept by faith that I am healed (right now) because of the finished work of Jesus. Lord Jesus, thank you for healing all my flesh and bones and taking sickness from my midst.

In the Name of Jesus, I command every sickness, disease, or demon to leave my body - NOW! And in the Name of Jesus, I command my entire body to be rebuilt, restored, and to function perfectly. Father, I thank you that (from this day forward), I am saved, healed, and set free! Amen!"

Stand On The Word of God

Once this prayer is said in earnest, you don't have to repeat it. You are saved, healed, and set free! Believe it and act as if you know you are healed.

Never be discouraged by bodily symptoms. Keep thanking God for your healing. Faith and thanksgiving release miracles. You may be healed instantly or progressively.

To keep your healing, cast doubt out and continue to praise Jesus for your recovery.

"For with God nothing will be impossible."

– Luke 1:37, NKJV

SUMMARY

*W*e can rest assured that we will start to feel better immediately when we know the truth (of God's Word) and boldly act on it.

How To Act On The Word of God for Healing

CAST OUT DEMONS – Say, "In the Name of Jesus, I command every illness, sickness, disease, pain, ache, and demon to leave my body now!" Say this over your body as often as needed and speak with great authority.

SEE YOURSELF WELL – Decide today to smile more, look better, act healed, and refrain from thinking or speaking on negative topics.

MEDITATE ON THE WORD OF GOD – Recite your key healing scriptures over your body at least daily or more if needed. Memorize them or keep a list nearby.

SPEAK THE WORD OF GOD OVER YOUR BODY – When demonic defeating thoughts enter your mind, counter them with healing scriptures. For example, say out loud, "By Jesus' stripes, I was healed. Nothing is impossible with God!" Let your body hear you.

STAND ON GOD'S WORD – Don't give up, don't cave in, and don't back down. Instead, defend the integrity of God's Word until you have total victory.

REJOICE! – Keep thanking Jesus for saving you, healing you, and keeping you well.

Remember that faith without action is not faith at all (James 2:20). So decide today that you will release your faith to crush anxiety, fear, and pain!

Surely none who wait for You will be put to shame; but those who are faithless without cause will be disgraced.

– Psalm 25:3, BSB

Starting today, every evil medical report has been replaced with a praise report through our faith in the Word of God.

Nothing is impossible with God, and all things are possible for him who believes.

– Luke 1:37, ESV; Mark 9:23, ESV

ABOUT THE AUTHOR

*G*ail Marie King, MA, is an author, entrepreneur, speaker, and mentor called to ministry in 2009. She has earned a bachelor's degree in Counseling Psychology and a master's degree in Guidance and Counseling. Gail resides in Chicago, Illinois, with her loving family.

Other Titles by Gail Marie King
Available in Kindle and Print

In Hindsight: Words of Wisdom In Quotes
21 Insights I Wish Mom Taught Me
His Spoken Word: In Lyrics & Poetry
Is He The One: Be Guided by God In Love
Marry A Man Who Loves God & Adores You

See Amazon Author Page - Gail Marie King, for all published titles.

COPYRIGHTS CONTINUED

SCRIPTURE QUOTATIONS

Unless otherwise indicated, all Scripture quotations are taken from the King James Version (KJV) of the Bible.

New Living Translation (NLT)
Holy Bible, New Living Translation, copyright © 1996, 2004, 2015 by Tyndale House Foundation. Used by permission of **Tyndale House Publishers, Inc.**, Carol Stream, Illinois 60188. All rights reserved.

New International Version (NIV)
Holy Bible, New International Version®, NIV® Copyright ©1973, 1978, 1984, 2011 by **Biblica, Inc.**® Used by permission. All rights reserved worldwide.

New King James Version (NKJV)
Scripture taken from the New King James Version®. Copyright © 1982 by Thomas Nelson. Used by permission. All rights reserved.

English Standard Version (ESV)
The Holy Bible, English Standard Version. ESV® Text Edition: 2016. Copyright © 2001 by **Crossway Bibles, a publishing ministry of Good News Publishers.**

Berean Study Bible (BSB)
The Berean Bible (**www.Berean.Bible** © 2016, 2020 by **Bible Hub** and **Berean.Bible.** Used by Permission. All rights Reserved.

Amplified Bible (AMP)
Copyright © 2015 by **The Lockman Foundation,** La Habra, CA 90631. All rights reserved.

English Standard Version (ESV)
The Holy Bible, English Standard Version. ESV® Text Edition: 2016. Copyright © 2001 by **Crossway Bibles, a publishing ministry of Good News Publishers.**

Christian Standard Bible (CSB)
The Christian Standard Bible. Copyright © 2017 by Holman Bible Publishers. Used by permission. Christian Standard Bible® and CSB® are federally registered trademarks of Holman Bible Publishers, all rights reserved.

Made in United States
North Haven, CT
24 October 2021